MAGNITUDE

MAGNITUDE

Releasing the Power of Your Leadership Presence

BOYD OBER

President and CEO, Leadership Resources

SUCCESS
PRODUCTIONS

Lincoln, Nebraska

© 2016 Boyd Ober. All rights reserved. No part of this book may be used or reproduced by any means, graphic, electronic or mechanical, including photocopying, recording, taping or by any information storage retrieval system without the written permission of the publisher except in the case of brief quotations embodied in critical articles and reviews.

This is a work of fiction created to illustrate principles of leadership presence as taught by Leadership Resources materials, consulting services, and training programs. If you need help with you, your business or your employees, consult a professional in the area of expertise required. Any resemblance to actual people is purely coincidental and unintentional.

Success Productions
8535 Executive Woods Dr #300
Lincoln, NE 68512
(402) 423-5152
www.LRSuccess.com

ISBN: 978-0-9970763-1-8 (sc)
ISBN: 978-0-9970763-2-5 (Mobi)
ISBN: 978-0-9970763-3-2 (epub)

LCCN: 2015919565
Library of Congress Cataloging in Publication Data on file with the publisher

Printed in the USA

10 9 8 7 6 5 4 3 2

CONTENTS

FOREWORD

Magnitude: Releasing the Power of Your Leadership Presence will speak to leaders of all levels, of all styles. It will help them understand what it means to create, manage, and enhance a personal brand. It will help them become aware of how to leverage communication, strengthen poise, improve interactions, and live their values and priorities.

When leaders know who they want to be and create behavioral patterns that present their best, then things start to click, and they gain traction on their intentions.

Making this inward journey is not easy. Leaders need to have a high level of emotional intelligence—a self-awareness on steroids—so they can grow in their role to inspire, gain followers, develop courage and confidence, and practice transparency; these are key to leaders presenting their best.

Magnitude provides a story that draws any leader into this journey of presence development. As you meet the characters—Jack, Glen, Sondra, Tom, Kate, Maryann, Miles, and Laney—you are ushered into a fictional reality where you vicariously experience their intentional changes to become better leaders who impress others with their magnitude.

Boyd Ober is a leader devoted to "working on his inside." Through our mutual connection with Vistage International, an organization that provides private advisory boards for CEOs, I've come to know his intuitive spirit that connects immediately with the leader within.

Boyd's book resonates with anyone interested in progress. Boyd has an amazing gift to combine vision with heart, execution with purpose, and relationship with communication. This gift shows up in all areas of his life—not just business but at home, in his community, and among his peers. He understands growth, emergence, and the support one needs to stretch into new thinking. He gets it. He works it. He models it, teaches it, and coaches others embracing the journey. And now he shares his magnitude of vision through this book.

Cathy Fitzhenry
Chairman, Vistage International–Omaha

INTRODUCTION

Leader, you are visible. And what you do through your visibility impacts everyone around you.

My guess is that you didn't wake up this morning wishing to slack off. You got up, determined to make a difference—to inspire, motivate, and invest in others. That's what you do when you're a committed leader. That's how you build a legacy. Your thoughts influence your behavior, and your behaviors directly influence how others view your leadership capabilities.

When you take your visibility seriously—when you choose to *develop your presence as a leader*—you transform the world.

Yet transformation of thoughts and behaviors takes time because the development journey is about progress, not perfection. It's about seeking those slight edge improvements that lead to new levels of success, again and again—to reach a magnitude that empowers your culture.

As CEO of a leadership development firm, I have been and continue to be fortunate to work with many successful leaders. I watch them to see what makes them tick. I coach them, challenge them, encourage them, and imitate them. I carry their challenges around with me for further study and pay attention to patterns that crop up in virtually every industry. I value and celebrate the impact these revered leaders have on those around them. And what I've noticed is a paradox. It's fairly simple to recognize the high quality of pivotal leaders when we experience it, but the mechanics of their greatness can elude us if we're not paying attention. If we're not paying attention to how they present themselves, whole and down deep, then what?

Why is that? Is it that our understanding of greatness has changed? Are we measuring their efficacy in different ways? Are fewer leaders accepting the invitation to greatness and rising to the challenge? Yes and no. The means of diagnosing inspiring leaders hasn't changed, per se; however, the information available to gauge their quality surfaces at an alarming rate. With a nose for news in this information age, we can find out more than we want or need to know about any successful individual.

Consider, then, the information others could find about you. Think about the testimony they would give on your behalf and the words they'd use to describe what matters most to you. Ask yourself if what others find or say speaks to the quality of how you want to be known.

Your presence is the persona you project to others through your behavior; you are largely in control of how others perceive you—of what will weigh heaviest in their memory of you. And this is nothing new. For centuries, leaders have been applauded for achieving tremendous feats, but those of leaders with glaring character flaws pale in comparison to waves of change accomplished through revered leaders.

As a business owner, a developer of people, a coach, I love to work with individuals driven for success. Yet leaders' drive for success—when unchecked—can veer them off-course for becoming the leader they want to be. May we never be too busy to develop what matters, what lasts over time, what defines our legacy beyond our "projects." May we find the time and desire to develop the wholeness of our leadership presence.

Magnitude: Releasing the Power of Your Leadership Presence illustrates the complexity and necessity of a leader's ability to establish and maintain strong, credible, lasting presence—to impress upon others a genuine distinction. Set in Seattle, this allegory tells the tale of Jack Geoffrey Merton, a financial executive, whose superficial presence almost brings about the downfall of an entire office until he and they learn how to develop a noble presence that lasts.

In this book, you will journey through a story that

- Teaches the essence of leadership presence.

- Unveils a signature style that attracts, appeals, and speaks quality.

- Showcases etiquette norms to demonstrate polish and convey social grace.

- Recommends tips for communication clarity and effectiveness.

- Amplifies leaders' seriousness and strengthens their reputation and legacy.
- Challenges leaders' values, virtues, and congruence that mark their character.

This allegory contains fictional characters with real strengths and real weaknesses—areas to magnify or improve through intense focus on leadership presence skills. Caught up in the saga, you will connect with characters who exhibit some of the same behaviors you might see in yourself and in those with whom you interact. Use the story as a mirror of self-reflection to identify areas of competency most relevant to your needs and circumstances. Take from this reading experience what will support the development of your presence.

Leadership presence—when done well—looks easy. But in reality, garnering respect, inspiring rapport, and gracefully executing—*that's leadership presence in action*—come from the fusion of competencies that can be learned and honed. If you want a respected legacy, build magnitude from the inside out, one behavior at a time. Cultivate leadership presence!

PART I: MAYHEM

1

DISCORD, DRAMA, DISSENSION, AND DISTRUST

In theory, Merton Financial owned the market. Everyone knew that.

A leading expert in wealth management, Merton Financial was said to have the best services, best people, best profit, and best potential. Jack Merton, president and CEO, had lived its slogan from the beginning: Make the most of what's yours. His multi-million-dollar company drew top investors across the United States. Being the best definitely fit its culture.

But best is different from perfect. And Jack Merton wanted to be perfect.

Rumor had it that a young, brazen Jack had lucked into borrowing money from his father's retirement fund to set up shop in Chicago in the spring of '85. A mediocre student at Loyola, he'd dabbled with stocks in college and knew enough to hatch a risky business venture. After his reluctant father gave in, Jack launched Merton Financial, and the rest is history.

Jack Geoffrey Merton had always had a way of turning the slightest edge into a significant advantage. What he called his "Midas touch," his paternal grandmother claimed to be more like sticky fingers. Regardless, those who knew him well said he had too much daring and too dead a conscience to fail.

But no one predicted Merton Financial would take off like it did. Within one year, Jack managed to open a second branch location in Highland Park, an affluent suburb of Chicago. Because he was savvy, he put the right people around him to work out the snags.

Within the next five years, three more prime locations cropped up in Illinois. And a remarkable thirty-some years after opening its first doors, Merton Financial had spawned twenty-seven locations across six states.

Somehow, Jack Merton defied all supposed odds.

～

From the outside, Jack appeared happy.

He attended the right parties, knew the right folks, and regularly pampered his wife, Sloan, who liked nice things.

He was living the dream.

At least, that's what Jack liked others to believe: that everything was going well and that Merton Financial was stronger and better than ever. Even when it wasn't.

And it wasn't.

The Seattle office had come to be a thorn in his side. And Jack was far from happy.

He preferred smooth and neat. And everyone else preferred that Jack experience smooth and neat. Since its opening four years ago, however, the Seattle office had been nothing but a fiasco. Discord, drama, dissension, distrust. Three general managers in four years equates to the exact opposite of smooth and neat.

From the get-go, Jack fielded complaints from long-standing centers of influence he'd tapped for feedback. How was Merton Financial–Seattle measuring up to the MF brand promise? His hopes for their references and testimonials disintegrated into sidebar conversations about how he might need to step up his game. Sloppy dressing. Poor customer service. Backbiting and detraction in front of clients. Incompetence. Inappropriate socializing during work hours. Stories of extracurricular activities running rampant. Had he seen them in action? Perhaps he hadn't spent enough time in this newest office. Such were the comments from secondhand, incognito sources.

The spewing he heard about from inside the office was worse. Hushed whispers, sidelong glances, toxic alliances, self-preservation. It was all beyond what he could touch or pinpoint. Elusive chaos with no clear head.

Onlookers say Jack's fatal flaw was bringing the second manager on prematurely after James Michaels left for health reasons. Maybe. But that didn't preclude the necessary firings of two subsequent incompetence cases or bear any weight in his evaluation of the current less-than-stellar manager.

It all made for rough, messy, and complicated—an incubator of imperfection.

And nothing made Jack as uncomfortable as imperfection.

But he was stuck. After all, there's not much a maniacal, sticky-fingered president and CEO can do with a mess he can't figure out.

The swanky steel-and-glass structure overlooking Elliot Bay in Seattle, the newest and most contemporary address for the Merton Financial company, was set to implode. It was only a matter of time.

That's why Jack called Glen.

Really, it was all out of desperation.

2

A Hard Pill to Swallow

Some occasions call forth heroic effort.

Glen's stomach dropped the morning he saw Jack Merton's call come through. Too many unfortunate dealings with Jack had conditioned him to expect the worst. Jack's call presented him an opportunity to start fresh.

He collected himself before picking up the phone.

"Hello?"

"Glen? Jack Merton here." Jack paused to clear his throat. He sounded on edge. "Been a long time, huh?"

"Jack, good to hear from you." How had Jack found him? It had been ten years. Glen smiled into the phone. "Yes, too long, Jack, too long. How've you been?"

In typical Jack-fashion, he bulldozed into the heart of the matter. "To be honest, I've been better, Glen. I have no time for chitchat today, so let me get straight to the point. I've got a problem I'd like you to fix."

Glen chuckled, relieved to be off the hook. "I think you have the wrong guy. I haven't a clue about financials."

Jack countered. "This is not about finance. It's about people."

Glen's interest piqued. He'd watched Jack run people into the ground over the years. It was only a matter of time before his tirades would come back to bite him. Their turbulent history of Jack screwing up and Glen bailing him out dated back to their college days. So what now?

He pushed himself forward out of his chair to close the office door. His left knee ached slightly from his long run that morning. He never grew tired of the thrill of lapping up the hills along the eastern coast, but years were gaining on him. He brushed the ache away to focus on Jack.

"In what way, Jack?" Glen stood in his favorite spot by the window. On a clear day, he could see the wave crests spilling along the Atlantic shore.

Jack cleared his throat. "It's the Seattle branch office I opened four years ago. It's been a problem from the start."

He went on to explain the brief history of the office, glossing quickly over the part about the three general managers and hitting extra hard the details about the rudeness and sloppiness he'd come to hate. Why didn't they take their job or the company seriously? They settled for mediocrity, with a good measure of sarcasm and spite thrown in. Not to mention—everyone was out for himself. But be careful about what you say. You never knew who would be running on oversensitive overdrive. And good luck finding someone willing to own up. Things had just gone from bad to worse. He'd done all he could do.

Glen could see right through Jack's veneer. "Jack, is it like this in the other branch offices?"

Caught off guard, Jack slowed. "No. Why?"

"I'm just trying to figure out if this is an isolated situation." Glen's calm irritated Jack.

"It most certainly is. In fact, you could step into any other branch location and see nothing but the finest people and service. But something ridiculous has happened in Seattle. I'm probably too close to the situation to make sense of it."

"What do you mean by ridiculous?"

"Well, everything I've already mentioned. Drama. People issues. Behavior problems. It's like nobody knows what it means to act like a professional. People are paranoid because no one trusts anyone else. And the past two quarters have shown a loss in profit. The problems are trickling into the books. I can't have this, Glen."

Glen thought for a moment. "What are you hoping I'll do, Jack?"

Jack presumed others could read his mind. "Fix it."

"Fix the people?"

"Yes, fix the people. Figure out what's going on and get 'em straightened out." Glen sensed a much deeper issue at hand and deliberated.

"Look, Glen." Jack picked up the pace. "I'm in my Chicago office now but am planning to fly out to Seattle by the end of this week and camp there as long as it takes to get the air cleared. Could you join me for a week or two? Take a look. Tell people to get their acts straight. I'm sick of dealing with this. That's why I called you. You're good at making people listen."

Jack waited for an answer.

Finally, Glen responded. "All right, Jack. I'll come. But on one condition."

Jack covered the phone, tipped his head back, and exhaled. "Great! Sure, anything."

"You can't be in charge."

"What do you mean?"

"I mean, you stay back and let me take the lead." Glen's voice showed no signs of budging.

Hands-off made Jack nervous. He stood up and moved behind his desk to face the panoramic window overlooking South Michigan Avenue. Chicago was beautiful this time of year.

He took a step toward the cool of the penthouse-office window, clenching his fist.

"Who's the one doing the hiring here?"

"This is about trust, Jack."

Jack gritted his teeth and started pacing. "Fine. Whatever you say, boss."

He slumped in his overstuffed chair and swiveled back around to face the office door. "Let's get you to Seattle as soon as possible."

"If I make some arrangements, I could be there as early as Monday."

"Monday it is. It's more than time to clear up this headache. See you Monday."

Glen hung up, dreading what was in store. Knowing Jack's propensity for being shortsighted, he presumed the Seattle debacle was the tip of the iceberg. Jack tended to rest complacent on the surface of most everything.

Heaven only knew how deep the problem really was. The acrimony Jack described among people signified many layers of conflict that very well may have been alleviated or even curbed by a more respectable leader.

Such as it was, Glen found himself yet again agreeing to help Jack out of a bind.

"No, wait," Glen muttered. "It's time Jack learned to restore himself." He reached for a yellow legal pad and sat down to scratch out some ideas.

∽

Later that afternoon, Jack sat at his desk, stacks of documents towering around him. He ran his hand through his coal black hair and sat back to loosen his tie. A striking man, he'd made every effort to look good. Flecks of gray sprinkled his neatly trimmed temples. He widened the neckline of his shirt underneath the loosened tie and smoothed out the tailored white dress shirt to adjust for a more relaxed look.

He felt ten years older than his fifty-one years.

The thin-lipped coffee cup Sloan had given him for Christmas three years ago sat on the far right of his desk. "Meticulous" it read in bronze script. Him to a T.

Some details he couldn't manhandle, however.

He picked up the spreadsheet in front of him, scanned it, and then dropped it back on the desk. Numbers didn't lie. While all the branch locations had troubling figures, Seattle was the thorn in his side; it hadn't held its weight from the start. None of this made sense. He was beginning to resent everyone involved.

Had Jack been a reflective man, he might have gone back to the beginning of the troubles—before Seattle's launch.

Miles, vice president of marketing, and Sondra, director of human resources, warned him about driving into the Northwest region without careful internal and external analytics.

But he wasn't, and he didn't. He pushed anyway.

To spite them, he'd grasped for the Seattle location like a man used to getting what he wanted. And he had no memory of his callous dismissal of their concerns.

No, it wasn't too rushed.

Sure, they'd be able to adapt to the culture.

Young professionals flocked to Seattle. They loved its thriving cultural atmosphere.

The cosmopolitan port city throbbed with energy. Of course they'd be able to attract the right people.

But admiring a wild horse is easier than riding one. And this past four years had been one long, rough ride.

This all left a bad taste in his mouth. Jack despised looking bad; he lived and breathed pretense. But scrutiny revealed something ugly brewing underneath the surface, a mess he'd rather brush away than uncover.

He walked over to the oversized map hanging on the wall of his office. Pushpins dotted the map at all twenty-seven locations. He located Seattle and circled the pushpin again and again. Bull's-eye.

He wasn't ready to quit. He turned his attention to tying up a few loose details before Glen arrived next week.

Time for Tom to go—branch manager number four.

~

Tom waited a full day to respond to the voice mail.

"Tom, it's Jack. I have something I need to discuss with you—something important. Here in Chicago. Call Maryann to get a time set up by Friday. It shouldn't take too long."

Meetings in person with Jack were never fun, especially ones he requested. Over the past year at Merton Financial, Tom witnessed Jack fly off the handle numerous times. He supposed there had been a somewhat good reason.

The situation in Seattle was deceptive. Within a week of taking the job, Tom regretted his decision. What he thought would be a dream executive position turned out to be a game of surviving the hornet's nest. Had he known what a self-serving, superficial CEO Jack would turn out to be, he never would have left his executive vice president position at the bank in Rochester. What an elusive, bungled mess.

The head hunter had said this was a plum job. Working for Jack Merton was equivalent to winning the lottery. He'd be a rock star in an up-and-coming company. Promises made during the job interview process never materialized. He could count on one finger the number of times he received support from Jack. Jack camped out in his penthouse office in Chicago and watched Seattle with disdain from afar. Tom hadn't been swimming with sharks; he was the bait. A far cry from rock stardom.

Tom glanced at the clock. Four fifty-five. He'd better get this call out of the way. He threw up a silent prayer and dialed Jack's executive assistant's number.

The phone rang twice on the other end. "Merton Financial, this is Maryann speaking. How may I direct your call?" She sounded as dull as he remembered her being.

"Maryann? It's Tom." He hated faking cheer.

No response.

"In Seattle." That ought to spark her memory.

Then came her deadpan response. "Yes?"

He imagined her sitting at her desk as he last saw her—thin lips pursed, fingers flying along the keyboard, ignoring evidence of any person around her yet uncannily aware of every noise and motion. Maryann found the world a burden.

"How may I direct your call?"

Something in Tom clicked. He had been in Jack's office enough this past year for Maryann to at least acknowledge him as deserving a less-than-canned greeting. He was manager of the newest division, for Pete's sake.

"Look, Maryann. You know why I'm calling."

No response.

He proceeded down the solitary road. "Jack called me yesterday about setting up an important meeting with him."

Silence continued on the other end. He swore he could hear her fingers typing away at the computer keys.

"So?" Tom persisted.

"So, what?"

"So what does he have available in the next day or two? The earliest I can catch a flight is tomorrow morning, putting me in Chicago by late afternoon. Could he squeeze me in?"

"The sooner the better. He said your appointment takes priority." She sounded put out. "I'll put you in his schedule for Thursday at seven thirty."

She sure wasn't making any concessions. "That's a.m.," she tacked on curtly.

"That will be fine. I can be there." He wished he could be anywhere else.

"Thank you, Maryann." His gratuitous remark did little to make a dent in her veneer.

"Um hum," she mumbled. Click.

This was not going to be pretty.

~

His airsickness on the flight was compounded by his lack of sleep. Nightmarish thoughts kept him up into the wee hours. He played through the entire past year at Merton Financial–Seattle.

What would he do if Jack fired him? What would he do if he didn't?

Tom Villamont, the fourth general manager of the Seattle office, couldn't pinpoint the core problem or its source. Was he the issue, or was he just the next sitting duck atop a disaster in slow motion?

Tom hadn't realized the extensiveness of the drama he'd walked into until it was too late. A teensy part of him ached to see it end.

He checked his reflection in the mirror of his hotel room. Tired eyes stared back. He couldn't afford to come across as more wrung out than he already felt. He inched down to the hotel lobby, grabbed himself another cup of coffee, pressed a to-go lid on top, and headed out to catch a taxi.

Ten minutes ahead of schedule, Tom walked into Merton's penthouse office in the Chicago headquarters. Overstuffed Ethan Allen chairs beckoned him in the lobby. As much as he wanted to sink into the security of the cushions and hide, he braced himself for the onslaught sure to come.

He walked into the atrium of the inner-office suite and saw Maryann at her desk, furiously typing. Already, he thought? At seven twenty?

"Good morning, Maryann!" He pretended to greet a friend.

Framed pictures of what he assumed to be her husband and children rested on the file cabinet behind her desk. He wondered what she might be like at home, with them.

Maryann glanced up to see Tom and then continued typing until he reached her desk. She spoke with her eyes on the screen.

"His office door's open. He's been waiting for you."

He stood there, paralyzed.

"Go on in," she said, as if scolding a dog.

And good luck, he thought to himself.

Tom moved toward Jack's office and entered, shutting the door behind him for what he knew would be the last time.

3

THE MIRACLE WORKER

Glen would have preferred a more modest entrance.

The spotlight made him uncomfortable, even though he realized others watched him—like a hawk—as he made his Monday morning entrance in Merton Financial–Seattle. The flight the night before was late. He'd almost missed his layover in Atlanta, only later to discover the hotel had overbooked and shuttled him to a budget hotel. It was after midnight before his head hit the pillow.

Tension couldn't have been thicker.

News had broken in the Seattle office about Tom's departure. He'd chosen to "explore other options" outside the company. His office had been packed up and boxes shipped out. And questions loomed unanswered.

An outsider in the office in the midst of unpredictable circumstances made people testy. Glen knew that. This wasn't his first rodeo inside the corporate bull ring.

Jack had done little to make Glen's entrance welcome, except for sending a hasty e-mail that caused more damage than good.

TO: All Merton Employees–Seattle

CC: Branch Managers–All Locations; Maryann Fitzmeyer; Sondra Pfeifer; Miles Daily

BCC: Glen O'Brien

SUBJECT: Special guest

FYI. Be aware that a special guest, Glen O'Brien, will be on site for an indefinite time beginning Monday.

I trust you will cooperate with him. He's here to help you get better.

If you have any questions, call my executive assistant, Maryann, extension 440.

$\sim$

As director of human resources at the Seattle location since its opening, Sondra Pfeifer prided herself on being a realist. Jack had handpicked her from his Chicago staff, and she welcomed the chance to have her own domain in the Merton empire. She thought her level-headedness her greatest asset. She could out-think and out-wait almost anyone.

The turbulence of the past few years had conditioned her restraint even more. Anyone expected to tend to the wreckage she'd witnessed in four years would be understandably on guard—heroically so.

But the current buzz about Glen O'Brien irked her to no end.

At seven thirty Thursday evening, the day after Jack's announcement, Sondra met Laney, director of financial analysis, for their weekly racquetball rendezvous at the gym.

As spoiled patrons, they usually had a court to themselves, but tonight, more racquetball players milled around than normal. So they ducked their way back into the hallway to wait for a court. Conversation turned toward the special guest.

"I heard Glen O'Brien singlehandedly influenced the cultural transformation of Brookfield Insurance Company two years ago and Cavenfield Bank of America a year before that," Sondra told Laney. "But who knows what he'll do at Merton."

"So do you think this guy's some sort of miracle worker?" Laney asked.

Sondra had liked Laney the moment she hired her four years ago for the analyst position at Merton. She'd come to appreciate Laney's frank and casual demeanor—a refreshing change from the cynicism spreading in the office. A single mom at thirty-two, Laney's natural drive just needed direction. Hiring smart people made Sondra look good. And Sondra could spot a winner, or so she thought.

Feeling safe, Sondra unloaded. "He's an unknown. Why can't we fix things in our own backyard? I've been involved in similar situations. Miracle worker? What does he know that we don't?"

Laney listened to the spiel, peeking into the court only once to check its availability. She volunteered a sympathetic smile.

"Why not give him a shot, Sondra?"

"What do you mean?" She didn't hide her deadpan.

"I mean, wouldn't it be unfair to let your previous experiences taint your impression of someone who is choosing to step into a messy situation? He must possess some courage." Laney swept her long, dark hair back and tucked it under her ball cap.

"Easier said than done."

A group of sweaty players came out of the gym, laughing. Sondra nudged Laney's arm and nodded in the direction of the cleared-out court. They headed along the back wall, Sondra trailing behind Laney's lead.

She spoke to the back of Laney's head. "You're not the one left to pick up the pieces."

Laney walked a few more steps before half-turning to wait for Sondra to step alongside her. "Look, I'm not saying your job's not hard or that you haven't had your fair share of bozos to clean up after. I just think you should wait and see what the new guy is like before you hang him on a pole. Who knows? He might make things better."

Laney had always admired Sondra's position at Merton. Plenty of freedom with little management oversight. She had been grateful—and still was—for the opportunity to move from a midlevel management position at a stodgy financial firm to the glass-and-steel Merton Financial world.

Sondra readjusted her gym bag on her shoulder. She was suddenly feeling warm. Approaching forty-five, she knew Laney, who was more than ten years younger, would give her a run for her money on the court. But that was nothing new; she'd learned to bear heavy loads with grace and grit. She didn't subscribe to the philosophy of doling out responsibility without taking her share. So who was this fixer, and why was he coming to Seattle?

"What do you *really* know about the guy, Laney?"

"Not much, I guess. Some people are saying he's a consultant of sorts who goes around fixing companies. I've heard he's nice, though, and I haven't heard anything overtly bad." She chuckled.

"Right. That's my point. We know nothing about him, except that Jack arranged it all. That's why I'm nervous."

Sondra pointed out an empty spot in the corner. They dropped their bags down on the court and started pulling out their gear.

"Chill, Sondra, okay? Let the guy do his thing. We could all use a do-over, you know. Come on. Court's ready. Let's get moving," and she trotted off to the other side of the court, racket at the ready.

Something was going to need to move, all right, Sondra thought. But not her. She wouldn't put anything past Jack Merton.

∼

Despite the awkward circumstances, Glen O'Brien seemed relatively unfazed. He chose to view people, in general, with the gaze of potentiality. He looked for what was yet to come. And what he saw came to life, every time.

For the first couple of days, Sondra managed to avoid the new guy.

Until he came to her door. "Knock, knock."

Sondra looked up from her report to find Glen standing in her doorway. No escaping now.

She'd seen him from afar at the staff meeting and in conversations with various folks. Nonetheless, she'd done her own searching on the guy. Laney had been right about his involvement in the Cavenfield Bank transformation. His presence emerged in an insurance company overhaul in Cincinnati, a real estate company acquisition in Dallas, and a dispute between managing partners in a Sacramento-based accounting firm. An independent leadership consultant affiliated with a development conglomerate in North Carolina, Glen O'Brien, it seemed, was an accomplished, professional hero.

But this was the first time their individual paths crossed.

And there he stood in the flesh, before her, smiling.

Glen in a basic navy suit jacket and tie—well-tailored and sharp-looking—exuding a quiet confidence she hadn't seen in the Seattle office for a while.

She tucked her hair behind her ears and stood. "Hello, Mr. O'Brien. What can I do for you?"

Her legs locked, and she wondered whether or not she should come out from behind the desk.

"May I?"

Sondra stared, silent for a second, unsure what he was asking. He motioned to come in; he was asking for permission to enter her half-opened door.

She stammered an affirmation, taken aback. She couldn't recall ever receiving such a polite request. He nudged open the door and moved forward in greeting, offering his hand. She came around the side of her desk and stuck out a stiff, sweaty palm.

"Sondra, thank you for taking a moment to talk with me. My name is Glen O'Brien, and—"

"Yes, I know."

He waited a second, enough for her to realize she'd interrupted. He closed his eyes and then opened them with benevolence.

"Your time is important, so I'll be brief. President Merton has invited me here to learn more about the people at Merton Financial."

She had to admit the guy was suave.

Sondra found herself half-listening and half-fidgeting. Standing next to Glen, she felt self-conscious and partially put together. Glen continued, overlooking her distraction.

"From what I understand, you've been here from the beginning and have hired most of the employees in this branch location, correct?"

This time, Sondra waited until she was certain he finished speaking. "Somewhat, yes. But all the previous general managers were heavily involved in the hiring process. I mostly worked with new hires after they had agreed to the job—or fired them, when directed."

Glen nodded. "Others speak highly of you. It's obvious they respect you."

She blushed, unused to compliments. "Thank you, Mr. O'Brien. I'm fortunate to work with some good people here. They deserve better than what we've experienced in the past."

She cringed at the harsh tone of her remark.

He didn't miss a beat.

"Yes, I agree. Back-to-back turnover experiences in four years bring lots of upheaval. Actually, that's what I'd like to talk with you about in some depth. Would you be open to meeting me for coffee this afternoon? We could meet in the lobby café. Even a half hour of your time would be invaluable to me."

The last thing she felt like doing was chumming up with the newcomer, even despite his charm and consideration. But he appeared harmless.

She stifled a sigh. "How about three o'clock?"

His face lightened. "Excellent. Thank you. I appreciate your willingness." He paused as if he were ready to say more but then turned and walked out.

She sat back down at her desk, aware of the impression his gracious response and smooth exit left upon her. A twinge of guilt burned her conscience. Why?

She did her best to brush it away and prepare herself for what lay ahead. Her resolve gone by the wayside, she'd been caught in a weak moment.

But Laney had asked her to give him a chance. What this meant for her she could only wonder.

～

Sondra sat across from Glen at the first-floor café.

Their chitchat had been light, simple enough for Sondra to scrutinize the celebrity. She found absolutely nothing to dislike.

But she'd been wrong before.

Nonetheless, she was intrigued. Something about him stood out—something she couldn't put her finger on. *Glen O'Brien wasn't easily forgotten. But why?*

In her line of work, she encountered people on a constant basis, and she had perfected what she'd come to know as the "positive-memorability factor." Did this person stand out from the crowd in a memorable way? In a positive, memorable way? More often than not these days at Merton Financial–Seattle, no one stood out.

Over the past few years, she'd projected frustration of others and their unpredictable situations onto herself. Here she was, director of human resources, responsible for grooming the professional representation for a company that lost its talent, and she couldn't put her finger on the pulse of their inability to retain high potentials.

She'd developed an eccentric habit of secretly rating people with stars based on the impressions they made over time. It was rather elaborate. Sondra visualized each person's image with a string of stars underneath. The more stars, the more positively memorable the person had proven to be.

It wasn't that she had a photographic memory; she just paid attention to people and their behaviors, unlike the majority of people in the Seattle office who seemed oblivious to the messages their behaviors sent.

She didn't like to think of it as categorizing people in a mental Rolodex; that seemed heartless. Rather, Sondra respected this system as her crutch to read people and peg red flags. But she just couldn't fix people problems.

And Jack was paying her to fix them.

"Right, Sondra?"

Glen drew her back from her daydream.

She shifted in her seat at the disruption. "Right, uh, yes," she offered and forced her mind to focus.

He leaned forward and looked her straight in the eye. "Let's get to the heart of the matter. What would you say is the biggest challenge at Merton Financial?" Glen leaned back and clasped his hands on the table.

Could this be a trap? Sondra could name ten problems off the top of her head with even trying. She hesitated to collect her thoughts.

"Mr. O'Brien..."

"Please, call me Glen." His offer was sincere.

"Um, Glen, yes, thanks. Well, I guess what I see as the biggest challenge is—"

She stopped. Here, she'd been looking for the chance for someone to finally listen, to hear her thoughts, her take. And now, she had the chance to lay it all out. He was waiting, as if he had all the time in the world to hear her answer, a most important answer.

She continued. "It would be discontentment."

His eyes didn't flinch. She mustered up courage to proceed.

"People aren't happy working here. They have no sense of pride in our company or our mission. I mean, many of them aren't even aware we *have* a mission."

Had she crossed a transparency line? She'd been more open with him than appropriate for a virtual stranger.

"And why is that, Sondra? Tell me what you've seen."

She thought for a moment. "I suppose the unraveling happened after James Michaels left four years ago."

She leaned forward a bit, noticing a hint of confusion on Glen's face. "He was the manager Jack Merton hired when he opened the Seattle office."

Glen nodded.

"He had a way of uniting us. We all knew where he stood, where we were headed. We cared and wanted to be a part of something larger than ourselves. There was something almost magnetic in his leadership. You could feel it."

"What happened after he left?"

"Nothing for a while. His departure was a shock, to say the least. His health had been ailing, and so moving into early retirement was a logical next step. Jack Merton believed in succession planning, but even best-laid plans can go awry when the ones who fill shoes are not up to par."

She took a sip of coffee. Glen waited for her to continue.

"A few of us tried to hold things together, keep the ship sailing, but it soon became apparent we were in dire need of a leader to keep things moving in a productive and profitable direction. Daniel Lewis had been groomed to be the next manager, but he had no stamina whatsoever—zippo, zilch. So he could hardly stand the pressures of the position. He lasted eight months."

She shook her head.

"Then Trisha Bennett came on board." Sondra paused and reached for her coffee. "She proved herself with a far too aggressive and unrealistic agenda, eventually driving many good people away. That was heart-wrenching to watch. And the last manager—the one here just before you came—Tom Villamont—nice guy, but..."

"But what?"

"He was definitely more approachable than Trisha, but he lacked confidence, which made him inconsistent and unpredictable. Nobody respected the guy. Don't get me wrong. They wanted to. He simply failed to gain their respect. He wasn't willing to address conflict, and he certainly couldn't stand up to Jack."

She cut herself off. "So there you go. That's our history. And now, you're here."

Sondra looked up with a smile, relieved to have laid it all out on the line. "What have you heard, Mr. O'Brien? Glen."

He stared at his coffee, tracing its rim for a few seconds before responding.

"Well, nothing, except for what you've shared with me. It's more about what I've seen. Since I arrived in Seattle, I have been observing everything and everyone here at the office. From what I'm picking up, the challenge is simple—in a complex kind of way." He took a deep breath.

"What do you mean?"

"This may sound odd to you. But it seems to me, Ms. Pfeifer, that the people of Merton Financial have not been trained to cultivate presence as leaders."

"Say again?" She leaned forward, not sure she heard correctly.

"Presence? As in clothing? No, Mr. O'Brien, appearance is definitely not the biggest challenge we face."

"Agreed, Sondra!" His face opened softly. "Let me explain. I mean presence as in the persona of every person as a leader."

"So you mean your own presence then, right? You're in this now too?"

"Yes, I include myself in the group, but I also include you and everyone else who works at Merton Financial. While each of us has a unique role, we all share in the responsibility of presenting the best of our company, the best of ourselves."

"Let me get this straight. You don't work here. But you're including yourself as one of us."

"Yes."

"And you're here to make us better, and you think our biggest challenge is that we're not presenting our best selves. Is that right?"

"Yes."

"What about the dysfunction, conflict, incompetence, not to mention the unethical behavior? Everything is so muddled here, Glen, and nobody seems to know how to fix it. I don't think paying attention to the way we present ourselves will even touch the problems." Sondra couldn't believe what she was revealing.

"True, yes. Of course, those are major issues that will need to be carefully addressed. What I'm saying, Sondra, is that tackling the presence issue should come first. It touches upon every other issue to some degree. I know this sounds hokey."

She mentally crossed out one star in his rating.

"Insane, more like it."

"Insane, nutso, fine. But go with me on this. Once each person works on developing a wholesome, believable presence, everyone will be in a better frame of mind to embrace the more complex challenges." He added, "If they still exist."

Sondra stared at him, incredulous, questioning how he could know all this in a couple of days' observation. "What exactly do you have in mind?"

His eyes sparkled. "I was hoping you'd ask."

Sondra waited for him to go on.

"Okay, then make sense of this for me." She leaned back in her chair, expectant, her hands cupped around the coffee mug.

He swelled with excitement. "Sondra, you know people follow someone they trust."

"Yes."

"And they trust someone who has earned their respect." He paused, looking for her response.

"Of course."

"That's what presence—well, leadership presence—gains. It gains trust."

"Okay."

"That's what's missing here at Merton Financial–Seattle."

"Trust?"

"Yes," he said. "Because of underdeveloped leadership presence."

LEADERSHIP PRESENCE GAINS TRUST.

She blinked a few times. "Pardon my ignorance, but you're going to need to explain to me how the way a person looks affects others' trust enough to cause the kind of upheaval we have in this office." Her patience waned.

"Look, presence includes appearance, yes, Sondra. But presence is more than appearance. And in case you're wondering, the problem in this office is deeper than you think."

She didn't respond, though she had much she wanted to say.

"What do you suggest, Glen?"

He was visibly relieved by her willingness to press forward.

"Time and training. I'd like to form a task force of key individuals where I can lay out the essence of leadership presence. Together, we could figure out what that means for Merton Financial."

"Are you thinking certain people from the whole company or just the Seattle office?"

"What would you recommend?"

She felt now was the time to be honest. "I'd suggest outside individuals in addition to a core Seattle team. Too much mud in the water here."

"Right. We'll begin with the Seattle office, but it would be best to pull in a few outsiders. I suspect we'll discover some systemic issues company-wide."

It was obvious he'd been thinking this through.

"All presence-related?"

"Yes. Simple and complex at the same time. No one is immune."

As if we've contracted a disease, she thought to herself. "I guess we have a lot to learn, huh?"

"We all do."

"If this presence thing is such a big deal, why don't we know about it already? And by the way, how did you diagnose us in only a week?"

She had expected him to laugh.

"It wasn't so much a diagnosis as a recognition of absence. I recognized what *wasn't* here."

He caught her eye for a second with unwavering confidence. "If you're patient with me, you'll soon see what I mean."

"I hope so."

She glanced at her watch. They'd been talking for ten minutes—remarkable ground in a short period of time.

She continued. "Who have you met who should be a part of this task force?"

"You, for sure."

They smiled in unison.

"Then Laney Richards, your financial analyst, correct?"

"Yes. Nice. A real team player. I'm glad she'll be included because too often she's overlooked."

"Why is that?"

"I don't know. She can come across as too casual, even unassuming." He reached into his inside jacket pocket and pulled out a small electronic tablet and jotted down a few words, then nodded.

"What about Miles Daily? Is he on your list? He should be."

"Miles, right, the VP of marketing. Is he the guy—"

She interrupted, laughing, "In the khakis? Yes, that's Miles."

"His image led me to believe he was an intern."

"He is youngish looking. But he can sure appeal to the hipster culture in Seattle. I think he has good insights to offer the group," Sondra suggested.

"He definitely needs to be a part of the group." Glen tapped out another thought on his tablet.

"Maryann Fitzmeyer." He threw the name out and looked at her face for a reaction.

"Maryann from the Chicago office? What does she have to do with what goes on here?"

Rubbing shoulders with Maryann was an unforgettable experience. On the few occasions she'd flown to Chicago to meet with Jack, she'd never once been made to feel welcome.

"Just go with me on this. Then Tom Villamont…"

"Tom? Really? They already cleaned out his desk! There's no way he'll come back—or be welcomed back, for that matter—for a silly task force." Delete. She imagined mentally crossing out another star in his rating.

He trailed on as if she hadn't spoken. "Tom," he repeated, "and Jack Merton."

She could feel her ears redden. The café grew uncomfortably warm. She had overlooked the slew of people coming in to buy a coffee for the ride home from work.

Glen was looking directly at her. "And me," he finished. "So that makes seven of us."

He'd laid it all out, perfectly undaunted.

She glanced around the room and then leaned in and spoke in a sharp whisper. "Are you intentionally starting World War III? Do you have any idea what kind of eruptions could occur with the personalities of those you named together in the same room?"

She pushed back in her seat and raised her voice slightly. "You don't even know these people. You've been here a week, and you think you have the answers to set us straight?"

His chuckle carried a serious undertone. "No, Sondra."

His voice dropped. "I'm intentionally setting up a conversation about behaviors, not personalities—a conversation that should have happened a long time ago. And I'm sure if you're honest with yourself, you'll admit that a host of behaviors have never been addressed. At this point, a stew of problems is so rooted in the Merton Financial culture that we have no choice but to begin at the beginning. That's why I'm here. To be *that* guy."

Touché! She didn't appreciate being scolded. But he was right. And she knew he was right. Any excitement she had felt initially was gone.

He let her sit in awkward silence for a few moments.

"When do you want this brouhaha to begin?"

He didn't miss a beat. "We'll need two full days, at least—possibly a third. The sooner the better."

He gave her another minute to process.

"Would you like to coordinate this, or should I?" he asked.

"Do I have a choice?"

He remained silent.

"Fine. I'll arrange it. We'll shoot for next Wednesday."

His voice was even. "Thank you, Sondra. I appreciate your willingness to do this without a clear sense of direction. Please let them know the two-day training will begin at eight next Wednesday morning. We'll convene at the front doors of Merton Financial–Seattle."

He searched her face. "Trust me on this."

"Yeah, sure." She visualized deleting two more stars from his rating.

One week away, she thought. Maybe that'd be enough time for her to find a new job.

PART II: MISSION

4

NOT EVERYTHING
THAT GLITTERS

Sondra took the elevator down to the lobby earlier than necessary.

She'd already put in two hours of work that morning, albeit unproductive work. She couldn't stop her mind from imagining horrendous scenes. "Don't anticipate. Just participate," she told herself, getting off the elevator and walking across the shiny marble floor to the glass doors.

Miles and Laney stood, chatting—Miles in a dark navy polo and olive khakis and Laney in a short, flared skirt and ballet flats. She knew both of them well enough to see they were nervous. Someone off the street would have thought they were a young couple waiting to meet with a financial planner.

Before she reached them, someone touched her left arm. Glen. He had escorted Tom to the group.

"Good morning, Sondra." He turned to face Tom. Sondra took her cue.

"Good morning, Glen. Tom." She gave a slight nod to Tom, overextending her smile to clear away the awkwardness. Tom, comforted by her polite gesture, blinked his sad, weary eyes. They passed idle time in conversation, until Glen looked at his watch.

"8:05. We're still waiting on Maryann and Jack."

"Speaking of..." Tom began.

"Ah, yes, coming up the walk."

Out of habit, Glen checked the time again and adjusted his suit jacket before heading toward the front door. On his way, he paused by Miles and Laney to greet them. Sondra watched Glen work the room. He indulged each person he encountered with genuine respect. His presence seemed to put them at ease.

The double doors opened, and Jack's bold presence filled the room. Maryann sauntered two steps behind him, her downcast gaze resisting eye contact with anyone. Her overstuffed purse haphazardly dangled from her hunched shoulder. It pained Sondra to look at her.

Jack hawk-eyed Glen and gestured him over. Glen obliged and bent forward as Jack sputtered into his ear. He reared back and looked Jack in the eye but didn't respond and then turned toward to the group.

"Good morning, everyone!" Glen said. "Let's gather over here by the side lounge area and begin our day." Miles and Laney moved first, heading for the overstuffed couch. Tom followed and stood behind a chair facing the street. Jack and Maryann stayed put. Sondra walked behind Glen, hoping her movement would spark Jack and Maryann. It didn't.

Glen motioned for them to join. Jack smirked and begrudged a few steps forward. Maryann shuffled over to the left of the lounge area.

Glen's clear voice betrayed no fear; he had stepped in front of the fireplace and smiled at the receptionist staring at him from behind the front information desk in the entrance of the Merton Financial office. He looked poised and confident.

"Thank you for coming today. I realize the sacrifices you have made to be here and appreciate your willingness to invest in Merton Financial–Seattle. And thank you, Sondra, for organizing this time together."

Sondra put on an obligatory smile. Except for an occasional glance between Miles and Laney, no one reciprocated his warmth.

"My name is Glen O'Brien. For the past twenty-eight years, I've been working in leadership development. I've had the opportunity to work alongside incredible people—incredible *leaders*—who were striving to become more productive, more effective, and more inspirational. So when Jack asked me to come to Merton Financial–Seattle to assist this office in developing its full leadership potential, I accepted, knowing the importance of the opportunity."

He continued. "From what I've learned about the Merton Financial mission and the culture here, there is much to be excited about. I've spent the past few days getting to know people here—some of you—and I see talent and energy and desire for excellence."

No response. Nothing.

"Anyone want to guess why I had us meet at the front entrance this morning?" Glen's eyes scanned one person at a time.

"So we can escape quickly?" Jack snickered and elbowed Maryann who glared back.

Catching Jack's eye, Glen recounted. "Far from it, Jack. We're here at the entrance—this beautiful, double-doored glass entrance—to remind us that what people see in Merton Financial is what people believe about Merton Financial. And what they see is you, each one of you, along with each person you influence."

Tom shifted his weight.

"That means," he went on, "that our presence—how others see us—is serious business. In fact, it affects how and why we do business and the quality that comes from our efforts."

CULTIVATING STRONG PRESENCE IS VITAL TO OUR PROFESSIONAL SUCCESS; IT AFFECTS HOW AND WHY WE DO BUSINESS AND THE QUALITY THAT COMES FROM OUR EFFORTS.

Jack crossed his arms. "Look, Glen, is this going to be a lecture?"

Glen took a step forward and stood tall. With soft firmness, he addressed Jack. "You invited me to come and see Merton Financial–Seattle, which I was happy to do. So what I'll share with you all today and tomorrow are the results of what I've seen and what I hope you will help others see."

Sondra smiled to herself. Chalk up one star for Glen.

Glen drew upon the warmth he kindled with Miles and Laney, who had softened already. Their smiles fed his courage.

"Today and tomorrow are about leadership presence. Not everything that glitters is gold, and not everything that flashes endures. Don't get me wrong. Glitter and flash certainly appeal. They catch the eye and draw attention. They promise delight and fascinate the imagination with mesmerizing charm like a stimulating first impression. But something more substantial is needed for a great impression to last. In other words, there better be something beneath the sparkle and shine."

Sondra scanned the group, searching for some sign of their reaction. They all shot Glen inquisitive glances. Where he was going with this gold metaphor?

"Take this gold, for instance." He side-stepped over to the gold-plated elevator, raising his voice so they could hear.

"Along with its distinctive sunshine glow, this precious metal is known all over the world for its purity, its density. Its value doesn't change over time. The gold standard surpasses the fleeting allure of all other gems. Why? Because of what it represents. Because of what's underneath its surface."

Even the receptionist stared at him, watching the show. He caught her infectious smile.

He returned to the group, a man on a mission. "We, too, can captivate others," he said while thumping his own chest. "We can use our charm and looks to inspire confidence in who we are and what we do. Smart leaders know this and use it to their advantage."

All eyes were on Glen.

He lowered his voice. "But it's the collection of impressions over time that lasts—that counts."

Miles interjected, "And not all lasting impressions are golden."

"Exactly, Miles. Please, would you share more of what you're thinking?"

Miles fumbled at first, disarmed.

"I'm just saying that appearance alone is not enough." His eyes landed on Jack who looked away.

"Agreed. Who else agrees?"

Sondra raised her hand, then Laney, then Tom. The receptionist behind the desk raised hers too. Maryann gave a partial raise, but Jack's arms stayed crossed.

Glen saw his window of opportunity.

"Appearance does matter, and we're going to talk about that. But like Miles said, more is at stake, and we need to talk about that too. Today and tomorrow, I want to unpack with you all the layers of leadership presence so that you can maximize your ongoing effectiveness as a leader and revolutionize the culture here at Merton. I think you'll be happy to know that things can be a whole lot better. Let's head up to the third-floor conference room to dig in."

"Excuse me."

Glen felt a tug on the back of his jacket sleeve. He turned to find the receptionist behind him.

"Uh, Mr. O'Brien, my name is Kate Hampel." She offered her hand.

Glen accepted her hand and gave it a firm shake. "Very nice to meet you, Kate."

She kept her eyes focused on Glen, ignoring the rest of the onlookers. "I've been overhearing your talk, and it all sounds so interesting. I was hoping that maybe I could join your group."

Her interest touched Glen, yet he could feel Jack's piercing glare.

Anticipating his concern, she continued. "Angelina said she'd be willing to cover for me while I'm away." Angelina from behind the reception desk gave a little wave.

"Pardon me for just a minute," Glen said to the group.

He pulled the receptionist off to the side for a brief conversation. Everyone else pretended not to gawk at one another until Glen's return.

Glen stepped back into the group with the receptionist at his side. "I'd like to introduce the newest member of our training group: Kate. She's the front entrance receptionist at Merton Financial–Seattle and has been with the company for one year exactly. She's interested in learning more about leadership presence. I've invited her to take part in our two-day training. After all, she is the first person many clients see when they walk through those double doors."

Jack shifted his weight and looked away.

Glen pretended not to notice. Instead, he escorted Kate to each group member and initiated personal introductions. Out of duty, the others obliged; they put their best face forward for Kate.

A twenty-something, Kate was a tiny, young woman in beige slacks and a leopard-print long-sleeved top that clashed with the flashy, green infinity scarf draped around her neck. Her dark eyes accentuated her fair, clear skin, framed by wispy locks from her short, blunt cut.

After the round of makeshift conversations, Glen announced, "We'll reconvene in the third-floor conference room. Once you're in the room, find a seat and make yourself comfortable."

One by one, each group member turned toward the golden elevator. Sondra moseyed over to Kate for small talk.

So far so good, Glen thought.

Almost.

"Glen, I'd like a word with you," came Jack's voice from behind.

Glen steeled himself for pushback.

Jack leaned into Glen and hissed. "What do you think you're doing?"

"What do you mean, Jack?" Glen played dumb.

"I didn't call you here to host a reunion and get everyone to play nice in the sandbox. You were supposed to come here to fix the problems with this office. An outside consultant. That's it!"

Glen paused. "But that's exactly what I'm doing. I'm addressing the problem. Well, actually, the series of problems."

"By talking about presence? What kind of malarkey is that? We've got turnover, incompetence, dissension, drama, not to mention financial troubles up the wazoo. We don't have time to worry about how people look, for crying out loud," Jack hurled.

"Jack, you trusted me enough to call me, right? I have no other agenda but to help your company be its best. I spent the last several days observing and getting to know people. And what I recognized were some areas to address that all fall under the umbrella of leadership presence. Besides, remember our deal?"

He watched Jack shake his head in amusement and asked, "Listen. Do you know what leadership presence represents?"

"No clue. But I'll bet you'll tell me."

Glen continued, ignoring the sarcasm. "It's everything, Jack—the whole package. Every little issue you mentioned on the phone two weeks ago can somehow be tied back to leadership presence. Honestly, people simply do not understand its depth or how far-reaching its implications are."

"You're going to have to do a heck of a good job showing me, then, because I'm not convinced."

"Agreed. That's why you are a part of this training," Glen said.

"And inviting Tom? Come on. What'd you do that for?"

"Tom has been a critical part of the leadership team for the past year. He'll provide valuable insight into the issues going on."

"He is or, should I say, *was* one of the issues, you mean!"

"He has influenced the issues, yes. And so have many other factors we'll be discussing."

Glen broke off and checked his watch. "Look, they're waiting for me to continue." He motioned toward the golden elevator. "Do you trust me or not?"

Jack gave him the once over. "You better not make me regret hiring you."

He brushed past Glen toward the elevators and hit the up arrow. The golden doors opened.

Glen collected himself before striding into the elevator.

Two full days ahead.

~

The light chatter in the conference room came to a screeching halt when Glen appeared.

He swallowed the dread stirring within him and approached the front of the conference room.

"Nothing like a little chill to get our brains going, huh?" His quip failed to lighten the mood.

Only Maryann responded. "It's always cold in Seattle."

Laney rolled her eyes. "Colder than the windy city?"

A few nervous chuckles escaped. Maryann chose not to hear.

Glen clasped his hands. "Let's get started, shall we?"

Jack maneuvered his way toward the back wall.

"Jack, yes, please take a seat there. Thank you." Glen even liked order. "There's a space for you between Sondra and Kate."

Even with his attempt to blend in, Jack's presence towered over everyone in the room.

Glen pushed through the anxiety edging upon him. He knew what he was doing; he was here for a reason.

"It's been my experience that most people underestimate the importance of leadership presence because they don't understand it. So I'd like to start by sharing a visual with you."

He reached for the colored dry-erase markers sitting in the tray and began sketching concentric circles on the whiteboard. As he drew, he spoke.

"For starters, each of you is a leader. You influence other people just by being you."

He walked toward Kate. "Kate, as the receptionist, you're a leader because you set the tone for the client's first and subsequent interactions with this office."

He stretched forward to tap the tabletop in front of Miles. "Miles, you lead a team in designing and executing marketing plans. Your leadership affects the internal and external message and presence of Merton Financial–Seattle."

He held out a hand to Sondra. "You lead all the employees in this office in regard to their human relations issues." Glen strolled along the table.

"Each of you is visible, and each of you is responsible for influencing the perceptions others have of this company."

Silence.

"Think of what you're doing to me right now." With a pivot, he faced them, smiling.

"You're watching me. You're trying to figure me out— to see if I'm legitimate, to see if I'm worth my weight." Sondra shot Laney a glance that said, okay, I'm giving this guy a chance.

"Here's another important point about leadership presence," Glen relayed, walking toward the side of the conference room where Miles was slumped in his seat.

"The people you lead want you to be present, to be *there*, with them—mentally and emotionally. They seek your wisdom and insight, seek to draw upon your expertise and humanness, to tap into your well of strength and courage. That's because serving others as a leader requires your physical presence—to simply attend to others in the moment in a way that demands putting everything else on hold. Leaders don't seek attention. They give it."

"Question?" Glen saw a hand in the air. "Of course, Miles. Shoot."

"When does a leader have time for all this... presence?"

"Good question, Miles." Glen sat in the empty corner seat beside him and faced the U-shaped group.

> LEADERS DON'T SEEK ATTENTION. THEY GIVE IT.

"Leaders make the time. They open up their own capacity to see and hear and think. They value being present, being with people, being accessible to people— you know. Connecting."

Laney stirred. "Okay, so presence is about being with people?"

"Yes, Laney. But it's more than that."

Jack exploded. "All right already! You keep saying it's more than what we think. What is it?"

Glen rose, shoulders back, his attention fixed on the whiteboard. "This, ladies and gentlemen, is leadership presence."

He extended his cupped hands around the diagram. The model contained five layers—one circle inside another. The outermost layer said *style*. Then came *etiquette, communication*, and *gravitas*. And the innermost circle in the model read *character*.

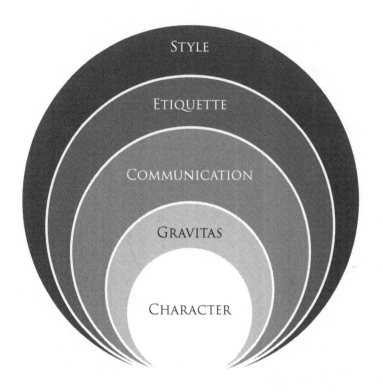

"The model is made up of layers, or parts, that form a whole package—a whole presence." He took a step forward. "When people see us," he said, making air quotes "they see all of these layers interacting."

He watched them process.

"So guess who's responsible for the leadership presence we cultivate?" he asked.

Silence continued.

"We are," Glen answered himself.

"Kate."

"Yes?" She blushed.

"Do you remember how you introduced yourself to me earlier in the office lobby?"

"Not really."

Glen spoke to her. "Kate's warmth impressed me—in a matter of seconds." He elaborated, turning toward the rest.

"She approached me, looked me in the eye, shook my hand firmly, and smiled openly. All of these gestures spoke to me. They told me she cared about me. And that makes for a strong first impression."

Kate smiled at the compliment.

"Making a strong first impression is essential to professional success because a striking impact is memorable. This first imprint of you remains in others' minds, making the first encounter a potential base from which all future interactions and opportunities stem. What will I remember about Kate now? She's kind, that's what."

Like five gold stars, thought Sondra.

Laney cleared her throat. "Mr. O'Brien, aren't we getting off-topic?"

Glen rolled up onto the balls of his feet and back again. "Actually, no, Laney. But thanks for asking. Something like a simple introduction touches upon the first three layers of the presence model in a matter of seconds. And yet, as strong as first impressions can be, they are not guaranteed to be lasting."

He steepled his fingers. "Think about it. We make rash judgments all the time that may or may not lead us to correct conclusions about people."

He's talking to me, thought Sondra. How many times had she hashed up stars too quickly?

"So," said Glen, "we need to consider the deeper layers of the model to develop a strong, authentic presence that lasts."

"Can you explain that some more?" Laney asked.

"Gladly! We can gain a more thorough understanding of people when we gather impressions of them over time. Likewise, what you do over time contributes to the lasting impression other people have of you. All these layers in this model refer to categories of behaviors or actions that influence how others perceive you."

Yes, Sondra covered her smile. That makes perfect sense.

At Glen's direction, Tom reached for some pads of paper resting on the table and distributed them. He then selected a green pen and passed along the rest of the colored pens and began jotting notes on his pad.

> WHAT YOU DO OVER TIME CONTRIBUTES TO THE LASTING IMPRESSION OTHER PEOPLE HAVE OF YOU.

Jack checked his watch and rubbed his temples.

Maryann crossed her arms, stared at Glen, and said, "In my opinion, this is all baloney. You're either someone others look up to, or you're not. Plain and simple. Some people are just luckier than others."

"I think you're wrong, Maryann."

Sondra typically never corrected people on the spot, but Maryann's arrogance rubbed her wrong. "I'm new to this idea of leadership presence, but I'll bet it's not about the luck of the draw. Glen, how does that work?"

Glen picked up his cue. "Yes, Sondra. Leadership presence isn't an innate gift that some have and some don't. It's the result of intentional choices we make over time."

He placed his hand on his chest as he spoke. "The good news is that the way others perceive us as leaders is highly under our own control. The bad news is that the way others perceive us as leaders is highly under our control."

Sondra grinned at the paradox.

Tom flagged a hand.

"Tom, you have a question?"

"Are we all shooting for the same goal?"

Laney interceded. "You mean, are we all supposed to be the same? Is that what you're asking, Tom?"

"Yes, essentially." They looked back at Glen.

> THE GOOD NEWS (AND THE BAD NEWS) IS THAT THE WAY OTHERS PERCEIVE US AS LEADERS IS HIGHLY UNDER OUR OWN CONTROL.

"No two leaders will manifest the same presence. And that's a good thing! You cannot be and should not be like anyone else. Your gifts and talents, personality and temperament, competencies and expertise, experiences and vision make your presence unique and unrepeatable. Developing your leadership presence is not about taking on a whole new you. It's really more about mining and maximizing the capability for greatness you already possess."

Miles looked puzzled. "Then what about meeting company expectations? Corporate codes of conduct and stuff?"

Before Glen had a chance to answer, Laney chimed in. "Sondra, do we even have codes of conduct or some type of expectations for leadership behavior?"

"Not formally. I've been meaning—"

"That's a problem." Miles interrupted. "We have the individual part down pat, but nobody knows what a real leader is supposed to look like."

Unruffled, Glen leaned into the tension. "Spot on, everybody. Established professional codes of conduct clarify expectations. That's a key first step. And within those boundaries, employees will find a wide range of free space for fostering a commanding, compelling leadership style—something that serves as a singular expression of all they have come to know and embrace as noteworthy and inspiring inspiration."

Glen surveyed the room and saw only blank faces. Jack was checking his phone for messages, and Maryann was rummaging around in her purse and pulled out a mint. Only Sondra seemed to be taking notes at this point.

～

Glen counted on time to ease the strain.

"Here. Let me offer one more thought before we dig into style." Glen sat on the edge of the conference table.

"Developing leadership presence is not a sequence of steps you'll accomplish once and for all. It's not like you get it figured out, and you're good to go. In fact, it's the opposite. Your presence as a leader should reflect the best of you in light of each new challenge you face."

He stood up and continued from the center of the room. "It requires an ongoing commitment to reevaluating your layers and the messages your behaviors send."

In all caps, he wrote on the whiteboard, *PEOPLE WATCH YOU*, and underlined it twice. "Your behavior is continually being analyzed, interpreted, and evaluated by others."

"No pressure!" Miles noted.

A few outbursts of laughter erupted over Miles's observation.

Kate ignored their laughter. "Mr. O'Brien, could we go back to the idea you mentioned about our behaviors having messages? What do you mean by that?"

"Of course!" Glen said, tapping his large Loyola ring on the table to punctuate his points. "Think of leadership presence as the image you project to others through your behaviors. It works like this."

He set his feet shoulder-width apart. "What we think affects what we do, and what we do is what others notice. If we want to change how others perceive us, we need to first change our behavior, but that requires that we also change the way we think."

No one's eyes left Glen, except for Maryann who sat back in disbelief. And Jack had retreated into a corner, absorbed in his phone.

Glen positioned a challenge. "Let's put it in more practical terms. How often do you approach someone, avoid someone, or watch someone because of the way he or she has acted or failed to act, which is actually passive action? How often do you find yourself imitating the mannerisms or phrases of those you admire?"

He walked inside the broad *U* of the table and looked each person in the eye as he continued. "How often do you consciously think about what you could say or do to make an impression on someone else? Answers to all these questions emphasize what you do: the judgments you form of others and they form of you are based on how you and they perceive and interpret behavior."

He punctuated his words with a pointed finger. "You, then, have tremendous sway over the quality of leadership presence others will attribute to you."

After some hesitation, Sondra asked her question. "No offense, Glen, but I don't see how we can control what other people think of us. Some people are going to dislike or disapprove or dismiss, no matter what we do."

Laney chuckled despite herself. "Yeah, the old damned if you do, damned if you don't thing."

"A valid point, Sondra. And, Laney, yes, you're right."

Glen grabbed a chair and rolled his seat closer to Sondra. "We can't make people perceive actions or intentions in a certain way, but we do have ultimate control over the consistent messages our behaviors send—messages fed by our thoughts, feelings, and beliefs—which we also regulate."

"Okay. I can see that. But, wow, that takes discipline!" Sondra said.

"No doubt." Kate hopped up to refill her water. "I'm not sure it was a good thing that I joined your group."

Kate's remark ignited a round of nervous chatter.

Glen spoke over the grumbling. "I commend your courage, everyone. It can feel daunting to think about how to behave in a way that affects others' perceptions of your competence and credibility, but after we've had a chance to touch upon all these categories of behavior," pointing to the circular model on the whiteboard, "I suspect you'll be empowered to project the best *you* possible."

He looked around. "Take a two-minute brain break."

Everyone stood to shake off the stupor. Tom pulled out his phone to check his messages. Engrossed in something, he continued reading until Sondra disturbed his focus.

"Tom?"

"Ah, hello, Sondra." He responded with genuine interest.

"Do you remember when Glen was talking about an organization's professional codes of conduct?"

Tom searched his memory to recall the conversation. "Yes, okay, yes."

"I'm feeling terribly guilty. That's something I should have…*we* should have done."

His vacant look confused her.

"Don't you think so? Wouldn't we have cleared up boatloads of chaos and saved time and effort and money if we had helped people understand what we expected of them as leaders from the start?"

"I guess, yes. That would have been beneficial."

"We dropped the ball, Tom. Or I did, at least. And I failed to build support—or, well, really, insist upon support—to develop others." She confessed more than she had intended.

"I hadn't thought of it that way, but you're right. But you're not alone. I sure didn't pick up the baton like I could have."

He let his sheepishness linger for a second and then questioned. "Why speak in the past tense, Sondra? I'm gone, but you're not. You're here and fully capable of turning this ship around, although it may take some clever work behind the scenes to get backing at this point." He tipped his head toward Jack's direction.

5

~

PEELING BACK THE
LAYERS OF LEADERSHIP

"Ladies and gentlemen, time to come back together."

Glen stood at the whiteboard with his back to the audience. He had taken the word *style* and drawn four rays coming out from the bottom of the word. Each ray was labeled: *grooming, dress, environment,* and *wellness.*

"We're ready to dig into the first layer of leadership presence."

Sondra reflected on Tom's words. She had a job to do. She sat back at her seat by the door, more alert than before. A cleared mind prepared her for whatever came her way.

Glen could feel the increased energy in the room. He used it to his advantage.

"Okay, a quick recap. Each one of us is a leader. We each influence others by our very presence. But here's the kicker. Our leadership presence is far more than our outside layer, just as a book is more than its cover. Let me ask you this. Who likes to swim?"

Only one person raised a hand. Maryann.

Jack came alive. "I didn't know you were a swimmer." She shrugged away his comment.

WE EACH INFLUENCE OTHERS BY OUR VERY PRESENCE.

Glen caught Maryann's eye and, with great delicacy, approached her. "Maryann, please describe for us what it's like to swim in a zero-entry pool."

Self-conscious at first, she began to explain. "Well, I would say it's glorious. The water starts off shallow, of course, barely skimming the tops of your feet. But with each step inward, the water rises higher, and the wading becomes more strenuous until soon, it reaches your chin. Then if you can strain forward one more step, your toes no longer touch the ground. You're buoyed up, consumed by the deep water."

She halted, uncomfortably aware of faces staring at her. "There's nothing else quite like it."

"Maryann, you have just articulated the essence of leadership presence."

"Say that again?" she questioned, wondering how her Thursday-night water aerobics class at the Y could have become a topic for discussion.

Glen stood behind Maryann and faced the group around the table.

"Inspirational leadership presence is like a zero-entry swimming pool. Picture this. The exterior appeal reflects depth below, just as Maryann described it. The layers of leadership presence flow together, conveying oneness—a mesmerizing wholeness enriched and empowered by its substance."

Maryann sat still yet raised her head and gaze as Glen continued.

"Anyone who looks at that pool or, better yet, swims in it, knows full well the translucent beauty of clear, clean water signals deeper, bluer waters—a sign of something more profound within."

She summed up his point. "It all flows together."

Glen punctuated her point with a slight tap on Maryann's shoulder. "Exactly. It all flows together."

Maryann's face broke into a smile.

Glen was on a roll.

"As Maryann said, we enter the pool from its most surface level. Similarly, your physical appearance is the first glimpse of *you* people tend to receive, so maximizing it makes good sense. It's their first experience with the pool. Yet swimmers know that the deeper they go into the pool, the more advanced their skills need to be. Likewise for leaders. The more expansive and deep leaders' responsibilities become, the more competencies they need to develop."

They were still with him, so he pressed on. "Leadership presence begins with crafting a style that attracts, appeals, and speaks to your quality."

> THE MORE EXPANSIVE AND DEEP LEADERS' RESPONSIBILITIES BECOME, THE MORE COMPETENCIES THEY NEED TO DEVELOP.

"Hey, Glen, sorry to interrupt," Miles said, "but I have a question. I thought you said that presence is about behaviors. Now you're talking about appearance. How is that behavior?"

Kate joined in. "Yeah, I was thinking the same thing."

"An important question! The short answer is yes. Presence is about behavior. The long answer is also yes. There is quite a bit you can do to influence the perceptions other people have of you based on your style."

He dragged a chair to the middle of the U-shaped conference table. "Your outward form sends messages to others about how much you care for and respect yourself, your position, and your organization."

He stretched himself back to face the whiteboard behind him. "Your leadership style is demonstrated through these choices." He pointed to the four rays under style.

"First is grooming. It refers to the way we take care of our appearance. And conscientious attention to your grooming shows you care to prepare. It makes you look put together. Take a minute to think about leaders you know who look well-groomed. What do they do?"

Jack, standing with the flat of his foot resting against the back wall of the conference room, proclaimed his opinion. "They understand the power of smells, clean lines, and edges. They use little touches to magnify the big picture."

He spoke like a man who didn't expect answers.

"Nice. Could you expand more, please, Jack?"

As if put off, Jack finished. "Everything is polished and in place, meticulous—everything: hair, face, nails, teeth, scent. Good grooming is a sign of class. It's what people remember about you."

Everyone in the room knew Jack meant what he said.

Glen rose with purpose. "Grooming certainly influences the visual impression of us."

He surveyed the room. "Let's try this. I'm going to move you into two smaller groups, ladies and gentlemen. I'd like each group to come up with a list of tips to improve grooming. Come up with at least five tips each."

He waited for protesting. "Questions?"

Sondra, Laney, and Kate arranged their chairs into a tight circle.

"Coming, Maryann?"

Laney's invitation stunned her.

Maryann picked up her belongings and shuffled over to the three women. Sondra scooted her chair over to make enough room. They exchanged a small smile.

The men, too, were congregating. Glen headed toward the back left corner of the room.

With palm thrust forward in protest, Jack refused Miles. "No, that's okay. I'm an observer today."

Glen swooped in.

"Actually, I'd like you to join the group, Jack. You'll offer valuable insight into this subject."

Glen saw Jack's jaw clench. He stood his ground.

After a reproving look, Jack inched a chair closer to Miles and Tom.

"Great! Okay, five tips, minimum, everyone."

Glen folded his hands behind his back and paced, shielding his grin from Jack.

～

Years of practice had conditioned Glen to coordinate different levels of energy. No one could have guessed he was sweating bullets underneath his suit jacket.

"Let's come back together as a group," Glen announced.

Conversations mingled as people turned their chairs around to face Glen.

"All right. Ladies, we'd like to hear from you first. List off at least five tips you identified for better grooming."

He knew if he waited long enough, someone would break the awkward silence.

Kate shifted in her seat, a reluctant volunteer. "I guess I can speak for the group. Should I stand?"

"Stay seated, and be comfortable."

"Sounds good," she said, looking at the group's list. "Well, we came up with nine tips. I'll just list them off, okay?"

She recounted their suggestions about hairstyles that frame faces, appropriate nail length and polish color. Laney piped into the banter, too, stressing the use of light makeup and the need for good dental care. Playful jabs peppered their discussion. Even Maryann took part.

Kate paused and scrutinized her small group. "Hmm...what was the last tip we had?"

Laney laughed. "Remember? We talked about making sure your scent doesn't stink up the whole room and gas people out?"

Miles threw out a smart remark for good measure. "Yeah, like Carla Mayer from accounting, right?"

Everyone laughed, familiar with the scent bubble she carried. Even Jack cracked a smile.

"A nice list to get us on the grooming track, ladies! Thank you."

Glen turned to the men. "Gentlemen, how about you? What tips did you jot down?"

Tom and Jack started to speak at the same time, but Tom stopped and gestured for Jack to talk on their behalf.

"Go ahead, Jack."

Blundering irritated Jack. He swelled with superiority and took the lead on the conversation.

"We came up with thirteen tips."

Maryann leaned over and cupped her hand to Sondra's ear. "I'm not surprised." Sondra returned a grin.

Jack pressed on, undaunted.

"Here they are, not necessarily listed in order of importance."

He proceeded with a litany of dos and don'ts, everything from how short a hairstyle should be to when and how to care for facial hair to the proper use of aftershave and lotion.

The group watched in amazement as Jack dominated the floor. He reminded them not to bite their nails, to avoid comb-overs; they should drink plenty of water and use mouthwash or breath mints, at least. A real man is a groomed man, he insisted. He rattled on until Glen pressed him to stop.

Jack sat down and tipped his chin back, ignoring his team members. "We could have come up with more, if we had had more time."

Glen nuanced the discussion. "Lots of good ideas to consider. You've emphasized the importance of taking care of our physical appearance. Again, these are daily health habits—choices and behaviors, if you will—that influence how you are perceived as a leader. But grooming is only one spoke under the umbrella of *style*. For the sake of time, we need to move on to *dress*. Go ahead and move back to your original seats. You may want to take some notes on the points I'm going to share."

As they were up and moving, Miles stepped into Laney's path and whispered, "This is the part I'm dreading." His smile covered the concern bubbling underneath the surface.

"Why? You don't want to hear you can't go hipster?" She knew he'd take her kidding with no harm intended.

"Yeah, kind of…"

"Oh, Miles, you're going to have to come to terms with being a professional at some point."

"I am professional."

"You know what I mean. Just wait and see what he says." Miles chose to follow her advice.

～

Glen was back up at the whiteboard again.

"Charles Dickens once said, 'Great men (and women!) are seldom over-scrupulous in the arrangement of their attire." In other words, it's hard to care too much about how you dress when working to enhance your leadership presence. What you wear notably impacts your professional style. It makes a statement about you and the organization you represent. In this case, the way you dress influences how others think you view Merton Financial. So we need to explore how vital principles in dressing for success can better prepare you to make first-rate decisions and boost your presentational best."

Miles raised a hand. "Can I ask a question before we get too far along in this discussion?"

"Sure, Miles. What's on your mind?"

"Okay. Fashion trends are constantly changing, right?"

Glen nodded.

"And Merton Financial–Seattle is serving a unique group of clients. I mean, face it. Seattle culture is all about the rave. We serve customers who are unconventional in so many ways."

"True."

"Well, so is this conversation going to be beneficial to us—to support our ability to connect with those we serve?"

Glen stood comfortably in the center of the conference table space, tailored and neat, someone used to being respected.

"Miles, I agree with everything you're saying. And given that, I would like to approach the dress question by presenting five timeless principles that can assist you in dressing for success. Of course, there are certain categories of dress, which I'll share with you, but these universal principles can be applied in any industry serving any type of client."

He spun around to the board and wrote *#1. Minimize distractions.*

1. Minimize distractions.

"Here's the thing." He began to pace.

"Others do notice what you wear and how you look, but your clothing is meant to be the introduction, not the conversation. Your clothing should attract and appeal in order to give your credibility a boost. However, your dress has lost its impact if it detracts attention from your personal brand. For example, excessive jewelry, loud prints, and low-cut blouses can detract from true professionalism. They steal attention and focus and weaken your message. Instead, let what you wear confirm your natural dignity and accentuate your essence, contributing to the pleasantness of your encounter with others."

"So this means we better choose wisely, huh?" Kate noted.

"Bingo, Kate."

Glen headed back toward the board. "Principle #2 is more complicated: *Fit the occasion*. Take a look at the handout I placed at your workspace when you were in your small groups."

2. Fit the occasion.

Everyone turned attention to the handout before them.

"Basically, every workplace has its own culture and professional dress guidelines, so adhering to expectations should drive your wardrobe selections. That means that as a professional at Merton Financial–Seattle, you are responsible for matching the dress culture here."

"What exactly is the dress culture here?" Laney asked and turned to look at Sondra.

Jack stared blankly at Sondra, so she proceeded. "Um, I would say we are business professional most of the time."

"We're business professional all of the time." Jack's correction hung thick in the room.

"We are?" Laney, shocked, pressed on. "Since when?"

"Since always!" Jack boomed.

In haste, Tom piped up. "Laney, um, I let things slip this past year to focus my attention on other issues. Dress wasn't something I pushed."

"You can say that again." Jack's mutter carried far.

Glen felt the tension rise. "Dressing for success confuses most people in most organizations. No wonder we're seeing differences of expectations."

Glen realized it was time to lighten the mood.

"Let's take a minute to talk about the four commonly utilized types of dress in the workplace: business professional, which we're saying is what's expected here, in this office. And then there's business casual, smart casual, and casual-casual. Now, keep in mind. The spirit of principle number two is to fit the occasion you are in— what is expected of you in this company culture."

He launched into the explanation.

"Business professional, which is what we are at Merton, is about looking as distinguished as you possibly can. It's the customary dress for industries that always demand professional standards, like finance or law or corporate settings. Formal occasions also require business professional attire—you know, interviews, meetings with new clients, special events where you represent your organization, that sort of thing. Basically, think white collar for the business professional. Those standards are fairly consistent across industries."

Kate had a puzzled expression on her face. "No one has ever explained to me what kinds of things I should be wearing. And I don't think I can really afford professional wear if it's as fancy as what it seems."

Sondra said, "That is our fault that we've not clarified expectations."

In actuality, Sondra assumed full guilt. "Glen, would you give us some guidance regarding what men and women can wear?"

"Absolutely."

Glen wheeled over the portable technology table and powered up the computer. "I'd like to show you images of acceptable business professional attire."

Once the screen was ready, he accessed images of business professionals.

"Men, we'll start with your attire first. As you look at these visuals, I'll point out some dos and don'ts. Okay. Notice the men wearing conservative suits—black, navy, or gray. See how the sleeves reach their hands? And how the pants match the jacket?" He flipped through several images.

> BUSINESS PROFESSIONAL IS ABOUT LOOKING AS DISTINGUISHED AS YOU POSSIBLY CAN. IT'S THE CUSTOMARY DRESS FOR INDUSTRIES THAT ALWAYS DEMAND PROFESSIONAL STANDARDS.

Miles in his khakis and polo shirt was certain he couldn't get invisible, much as he wanted to at that moment. He was the most underdressed person in the room.

"Also, you might have picked up on the fact that the shirts are long-sleeved and pressed. Button-down, collared shirts in conservative, solid colors are expected, gentlemen."

Glen smiled. "Of course, ties should accompany the suits. Try to get a quality fabric, like silk, and you'll want to make sure your tie has no spots. See where the tie lands—to the center of the belt buckle?" He used his laser pointer to show and tell.

"Don't forget the shoes either! A clean, polished dress shoe in traditional brown or black is preferred. Then a little secret. Coordinate your dress socks with your suit. Tom, do you have a question?"

"Glen, I've always wondered. Should socks match your pants or shoes?"

"With your shoes, of course." Jack shot out an unequivocal answer.

Miles looked down at his Birkenstocks and sockless feet. Oh, boy, he thought, I'm clearly not in this league.

Glen cleared his throat. "Actually, Jack, no. Match your socks with your pants. Lots of guys get this wrong. Any other questions like that? Now's the time to ask."

Tom added another. "Okay. What about buttoning a suit jacket?"

"As in when to button versus when to leave it open?" Glen answered without waiting for confirmation. "When standing, button either the top or top two buttons, leaving the bottom button undone. When seated, all buttons can be undone. Does that help?"

"Yes!" Miles and Tom spoke in tandem. Miles took a mental inventory of his closet and came up with exactly two suits and a sport coat. And he couldn't recall any dress shirts.

"Great," Glen said. "All right. Ladies, your turn. Let me open up a new folder here."

He navigated his way through the computer files.

"Once you see these pictures, you'll recognize similarities with the men. Here we go." He turned to face the images on the screen, drawing their attention with the laser pointer.

"Conservative suits, as well, are customary in black, brown, navy, or gray. Either tailored, wide-legged dress pants or suit skirts are acceptable—preferably in the same color as the suit jacket. Now, if you wear a skirt, it should come to the knee and cover your thigh when sitting. No slits!"

He pointed to a new image and reinforced the use of button-down, pressed dress shirts with collared or simple round necklines. "As with the men's guidelines, ladies, choose conservative colors. Business professional attire is a dignified, serious attire."

"Glen, what restrictions do we have on shoes?" Laney asked.

"Sure, Laney. Closed-toed, for one. Classic, low pumps are preferred, and hosiery or trouser socks are expected."

Kate and Laney shared their disappointment with frowns, and Kate said what they were thinking, "But there are so many cute open-toed shoes!"

Laney's eyes fell to her ballet flats, after glancing over the flared skirt that now seemed a bit too short.

"Then they would be better suited for business casual attire. Pardon the pun." Glen liked to jest. "Take a look at the major differences between business professional and business casual. To do this, it would be simplest if I marked down some general contrasts on the whiteboard."

$\sim$

Before he started writing, he faced the group. "I should say that the greatest latitude exists in business casual attire. It runs from anywhere a notch below business professional to a smidge above casual-casual—and everything in between. So here again I will reinforce principle number two: fit the occasion!" He went back to writing.

"Here we go." His voice held a touch of concern.

"Before I share these, I have to iterate the looseness of business casual guidelines. Business casual does not mean you can wear whatever you want; rather, it's about looking professional in a comfortable way. Think of it as preserving a sophisticated presence without the suit. Business professional follows fairly stable, traditional guidelines. But business casual offers a wide berth of options, ultimately decided by the particular organizational culture. So these are some general differences I see."

He bulleted the points as he wrote and read them aloud:

- "Suits are not necessary in business casual, but suit jackets can be quick items to throw on, making you business-ready.

- "Colors of shirts and pants do not have to be the same color.

- "Dockers, khakis, or dress pants can be worn instead of suit jacket pants.

- "And for women, flats and certain (dressy!) open-toed shoes could be acceptable."

He turned to the group. "So let's talk about these, shall we?" He moved toward Miles.

"Miles, you seem to favor khakis. But if you had a nice sports coat hanging on the back of your office door, you'd be business-ready, as long as you were wearing a nice pressed shirt." Glen didn't wait for Miles to respond before he moved on to Sondra.

"Now, Sondra is wearing low heels. Perfectly acceptable for business professional and business casual. But she needs to wear stockings to truly be professional." Sondra's ears turned crimson.

Glen turned his attention to Maryann. "Maryann, a sleeveless top detracts from your professional image. May I suggest you go with something less intense and smarter, with at least sleeves that cover your upper arms? Your jewelry is fine for other occasions, but the necklaces make too much noise when you move; that can easily distract people. Simple gold hoops and one tasteful neck chain could complement a toned-down top. Even accent it." Maryann scowled and crossed her arms, caressing the bare flesh.

"So, what questions do you have before we move on to the last three timeless principles?" Glen stepped out in front of the podium, eager to move on.

Chatter broke out amid the groups.

Kate started. "Yeah, I've heard some people talk about smart casual. What is that, and when do we dress in that way?"

"I've wondered the same thing," said Miles.

"Yes, good to know. In general, smart casual is a neat, conventional style that merges business professional and business casual—a step between them really. Its goal is to make you look smart and well-pulled together. However, it comes with a warning. Smart casual requires a fashion know-how to create a personal style with features from professional and casual attires—to know what to mix with what: suit jackets and dark pants, stylish sweaters and leather boots, vests and khaki pants. You know, it's the academia meets conference attire, daring to be vogue."

"Oh, Miles, you better not try it!" Only Laney could tease Miles without his taking offense.

"I'm lucky to find clean pants in the morning," he quipped.

Maryann moved ahead, serious. "You mentioned a fourth type of attire?"

Glen shook his head. "Right. Casual-casual. Merton Financial–Seattle doesn't lend itself to this type of dress—T-shirts, jeans, shorts, tennis shoes, or even sandals—relaxed standards, obviously. Jack made that clear earlier."

"Ahh....too bad." Everyone laughed at Miles but Jack.

Jack's icy voice cut the fun. "I haven't yet seen the business professional standard met here consistently."

Everyone clammed up.

Glen checked his watch. "Wow. It's time for another quick break. This is what I'd like us to do. Take five, and when you get back, we'll finish up the outermost layer of style. By then, it will be time for lunch—a working lunch. Okay? Five quick minutes. See you back at ten fifty-five."

Glen needed to collect his thoughts and refresh his memory as to why he agreed to help Jack Merton in the first place. He stepped into the hall.

Miles slipped out after him.

"Glen," Miles called out. Hoping to catch Glen alone, he hustled forward for a private conversation.

Glen turned to see Miles approaching and stopped.

"You and Jack seem to have a history." Miles figured he might as well be forward.

"We go back a ways, yes," Glen said.

Pressing further, Miles said, "So what's the story?"

"We worked together at Flynn Scott Wealth Management, where he was vice president of investor relations, and I handled corporate training. But that was more than twenty years ago. We were young. His path took him one way and mine another."

"So you're friends?" Miles pursued.

"We were. Now I'm trying to bail him out of a bad situation here. He trusts me enough with this task."

"But not really?"

"He knows I can do the job. Let's say I'm not on his Christmas card list every year." Glen smiled and started walking back toward the conference room.

Miles's voice followed him. "But what's between you two?"

Glen stopped and waited for Miles to reach him.

"We didn't see eye to eye on how to motivate people to be their best."

Miles grinned. "So maybe he asked you to come here because he found out his way doesn't work."

"Maybe." Glen returned the grin and headed back into the room.

~

Friction lingered even after the break.

Glen hoped a few minutes of stretching would clear the air. But a pompous Jack stood in his usual place by the back window, absent-mindedly searching his phone. Laney and Kate entered the conference room from break speaking in voiced whispers, and Miles and Tom sat more somber than ever. Maryann flitted her eyes between watching the movements in the room and randomly flipping through the handouts. Only Sondra sat attentive and ready for the ongoing lesson.

She caught Glen's eye and gave him a nod as if to say, "Go ahead. I have your back." He returned her support with a knowing look.

"We're back with lots to do. To refresh your memory, I'm directing your attention back up to the board where you'll see the first two timeless principles for dress: number one is minimize distractions and number two is fit the occasion. I'd like to introduce number three, which is *invest in essentials*. Would anyone like to venture a guess as to how this principle applies across all industries and all types of attire?"

Sondra jumped in. "Well, I think Kate touched upon it earlier. She mentioned being unable to afford a lot of the expensive items expected with a business professional wardrobe. Perhaps this principle reminds us that we can be smart about our purchases in order to look good while remaining fiscally sound."

3. Invest in essentials.

"Now that I think about it," Kate said, "with a little planning and selective searching, it is possible to build a strong wardrobe base that can be expanded easily. Laney and I were just talking about this very thing at break."

Kate touched Laney on the arm. "Would you share with the group what you told me?"

Laney felt a little awkward taking center stage. "Kate's giving me more credit than I deserve, especially since I've not been dressing up to par myself."

She glanced over at Tom, too scared to peek back at Jack. "When you were talking, Glen, I was thinking about people in our office who always look put together—like Sondra. And I was making lists in my head of what they wear and don't wear while visually running through the items in my closet at home. If I could buy a few key pieces, I'd give my wardrobe a jump-start into full functioning professional attire. You know, like a classic black blazer that I could throw over a dress, or a crisp, white, button-down shirt—"

"And outerwear. Appropriate in Seattle," Maryann interrupted. "You'd want one of those for luncheon meetings."

"Yes, you're right, Maryann. Thanks." Laney threw Maryann a grateful look.

Glen continued the conversation thread. "Might I also add a good black dress and a silk or cashmere sweater set and a comfortable set of black pumps?"

The women nodded in agreement.

"And for men?" Tom, once again, advanced the discussion.

"Yes, thank you. Men, if you could purchase a couple of long-sleeved, collared dress shirts in conservative colors, a couple of good quality suits, a pair or two of black or brown dress shoes, and a tailored overcoat, you'd be set." They returned his gaze blankly.

"Think of it this way. Dressing for the job you want, not the job you have is a mindset to keep you motivated to build your wardrobe one piece at a time. These things take time."

Glen walked toward the edge of the conference table and sat down. "Principle number three makes the most sense when we realize that our attire supports our professionalism. And leaders must be professional. Remember, others watch you. They judge your credibility based on what you demonstrate."

The blank stares signaled to Glen that they weren't convinced.

Glen surveyed the room and steeled himself to go on.

"I'd like the group's help for the next principle. By tapping into your prior experiences, you can explain number four: *Accessorize tastefully*. It's similar to principle number one, which is minimize distractions, but it deals with how to appropriately finish off a polished look.

"You've probably all heard of the power of simplicity. Yes? Take a minute to close your eyes and recall accessories you've seen others wear that detract from their polished look. When you think of something, please share."

He gave them a few minutes to quietly reflect.

Kate started. "I think accessories make the outfit. They really let your personality shine through."

Remembering the earlier admonishment about her jewelry, Maryann shook her head. "Yes, but you have to be careful not to overdo it."

"Oh, I know. I'm just saying…" Kate replied with hesitation.

"Wait a sec, Maryann," Miles said. "What would you call overdoing it? Can you give us an example?"

"Well, I see gals coming into the office wearing dangling earrings, necklaces, bracelets, rings, belts, scarves, glasses—all at the same time. That's too much!" Maryann, hearing her own dangling earrings tinging, stopped speaking and swallowed hard.

Glen stepped into the conversation carefully. "Maryann and Kate both raise valid points. Signature style pieces do give a spritz of personality. But a little can go a long way. A few smartly chosen accent pieces do wonders. When it comes to accessories, most of the time, less is more."

"So, Glen, can you offer some concrete guidance on this? I mean, taste differs, right?" Laney asked.

"True, Laney, true. Here are a few general guidelines that give our conversation some context."

Glen headed back to the whiteboard to jot down his thoughts, and the group picked up their pens to take notes.

"Generally," he said, gesturing with one finger, "appropriate accessories for business attire include simple, basic jewelry rather than dangling or flashing jewelry—like earrings or bracelets. Silk scarves make an attractive addition, and women should stick to closed-toed shoes and stockings with skirts and dresses."

He surveyed the room and saw only heads down notetaking, except for Jack. He was now texting and didn't look up.

"Men, as well, have some loose expectations," Glen went on. "For example, they may want to invest in a good leather wallet. And they will also want to get in the habit of wearing long dress socks as opposed to short socks—always matching nice quality socks with pants and matching belts with their shoes. I would also suggest, men, that you wear an undershirt with your button-down shirts."

Glen noticed Tom fidget, as if he wanted to speak. "Tom? You look like you had a thought you'd like to share."

"I guess it's more of an opinion. Well, I want to be delicate in how I phrase this, but I've always thought it more professional to cover any tattoos or body piercings."

"Agreed!" Jack's boom torpedoed over their heads. The severity of his reaction is what surprised others. Learning what would bristle Jack was disconcerting.

Glen took the opportunity to pull him into the group's conversation. "Jack, please tell us more about this."

Jack hurled into a tirade about impeccability. Merton Financial employees were to be impeccable, to look the part of the quality they represented, to make clients proud to be associated with Merton Financial.

He rang out his last thought. "And tattoos and body piercings flaw that image."

No one spoke. They could see how adamant Jack was about his position. Who would dare contradict the president of the company about something he obviously felt so strongly? It was his prerogative, after all.

Miles inched down farther in his seat. He was glad his polo shirt covered the tattoo on his left bicep. Only Sondra knew he had gotten it while serving in the military in Iraq, a short stint in the army after high school.

After a few seconds of silence, Glen addressed the group.

"Thank you for sharing your perspective, Jack."

There was only so much softening Glen could do.

～

After a quick stretch break, they sat themselves back at the table, except Jack who had pulled a chair to the far back corner. He pretended to be engrossed in reading his e-mails.

Glen was finding it easier to overlook Jack. He smiled broadly at the group.

"All right. Let's move onward. We have one more timeless principle to guide our understanding of business attire. Number five is *be modest.*" He wrote it on the whiteboard before leaning both hands on the table in a strong, assertive pose.

"Like the other four principles, this one applies whether your organization requires business professional or allows casual-casual. More than anything, your dress should respect the dignity of you and those who see you. And clothing that detracts from your value as a person—a person with principles, intelligence, talents, and heart—works against the leadership presence that will inspire others to greatness."

Glen's face and tone grew serious.

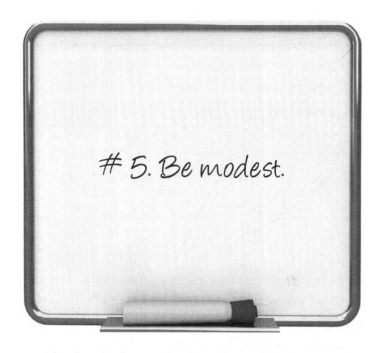

5. Be modest.

Glen brushed away the fear of sounding preachy. "All of us—men and women—are responsible for promoting modesty in the workplace. And that starts with an appreciation for each person and extends to a healthy respect for attire that promotes mental, emotional, and spiritual well-being. And then we have to clarify expectations and hold people accountable to them."

Sondra looked away, her mind elsewhere.

"I know this feels uncomfortable to talk about, but it's necessary." Glen sat down at an empty chair, seating himself at the U-shaped table. He leaned forward and addressed the group frankly. "When clothing reveals excessive skin or hugs curves tautly or draws attention away from the face or stretches tightly against body parts, modesty is at risk. This can lead to distraction, unprofessionalism, and, over time, a lack of confidence and self-worth."

Everyone but Sondra stared at him; she was too busy thinking of all the immodest dress she'd chosen to overlook. Not hers, but other employees. The cropped camisole worn by the new hire in sales. Every time she lifted her arms, her belly-button piercing showed. Then there was the financial consultant who, unknowingly or not, revealed way too much cleavage with low-cut blouses. Okay, she decided, it was knowingly. And she was kicking herself for not saying something to the accounting intern; his shirts were far too tight. No need to parade his biceps.

> MORE THAN ANYTHING, YOUR DRESS SHOULD RESPECT THE DIGNITY OF YOU AND THOSE WHO SEE YOU.

"A positive way to present this to those we lead is to reassure them that modesty doesn't mean boring or bland. On the contrary, tastefully modest dress demonstrates self-composure, authentic confidence, and high regard for your leadership responsibilities," Glen said.

Tom added after careful thought. "I guess we could say that principle number five helps everyone concentrate on what matters most."

"Nicely put, Tom."

All but Jack acknowledged Tom's remark. Jack was preoccupied with doodling in his notebook, having apparently tuned out the group.

～

A sense of urgency increased.

Glen tapped out a drumbeat on the table and fired up. "Grab a bottle of water, if you wish. We still have some chilling in the refrigerator, and let's move on to the third component of style."

He said, "I'd like to try something. I want each of you to go back to your desk or office space and take a good look around. Take a mental snapshot of what you see. Pay attention to what's on the desk, computer, on any shelves, in the trash. Whatever you see. In other words, check out your workspace. Then be prepared to share the results with the rest of us. Questions?"

"This ought to be fun." Miles joked to no one in particular.

"And, Tom, why don't you look around at someone's work environment. Maybe you could wander into the cubicle area."

"Sure," Tom said, reluctant to mingle with employees who were under his leadership just a week earlier.

"Do you need some help finding your office, Miles?" Laney began pushing chairs in.

Glen chuckled and waited until the majority of the group left before catching Sondra.

"Sondra, could I speak with you a minute?"

She had stayed put, absorbed in the notes she'd taken.

"I couldn't help but notice a change in your demeanor. Is there something you'd like to talk about?"

Sondra looked tired. "Oh, I'm just trying to process this all. I mean, well, none of it's rocket science. So how come I didn't know enough to hold people accountable to such simple yet important expectations?"

Glen sat beside her. "Time for a little perspective, Sondra. We're only on the first layer of presence."

"I know! That's what makes me nervous. How much more have I neglected? I don't even know what I don't know."

"Or…how much do you have *right*? Sondra, I wasn't called here to fix you. I was called here to support you in supporting others. And I can assure you that there's a great deal you're doing quite well—exceptionally well, in fact."

She peeked up right as Kate and Tom came into the room, chatting. The others trickled in, with Jack lagging behind carrying a hot coffee he purchased from the café.

"Thank you for listening, Glen. I'm enjoying what we're learning and appreciate having your help," Sondra said.

Her warm smile encouraged him.

Some things were moving in the right direction.

～

"So what did you see?" Glen asked.

They all started talking over one another. Kate's voice won out first.

"I hate to admit it, but my desk could be so much neater! I had a couple of pop cans sitting out, files in various stacks, and Post-it notes all over the place. But I'm really glad I looked because something clicked for me. I'm the first person people see when they walk into our building, and my desk is not sending the message of impeccability Jack talked about."

"Thank you for your honesty, Kate. Others? What did you see?" Glen asked.

Maryann added her commentary, unabashed. "Well, obviously, my desk is not in this office building, so I toured the floor, looking around at other workspaces. A few were neat, but the majority of them were overflowing with stacks of papers and folders and, frankly, junk. It was suffocating! I don't know how anybody can get anything done in those circumstances. Maybe it's just me, but I think there's a lot of room for change here."

"Now, wait a minute. I take that personally." Miles feigned heart pain. "True, my desk could be neater, but it doesn't affect my productivity."

"I think what Maryann is implying here is that neat and clean personal spaces tell observers you value order and respect those who enter them," Glen said. "Others gain more confidence in your professionalism when they see your meticulous care of details. They attribute pleasing environmental appearance to your character and are more likely to trust your ability to produce results. In addition, you will feel better when your surroundings are organized and clean—everything is in its proper place."

The group agreed, fully aware that what Glen clarified sounded nothing like what Maryann had said.

He felt it best to move on. "May I add one more piece to style, the outmost layer of leadership presence?"

"Sure. We're up for it." Laney's chirp lightened the mood.

"Great."

Glen grabbed a chair and sat it in front of the group, at the head of the table. "It's wellness."

Kate let out a squeal. "This is right up my alley! I am an unbelievable health nut. In fact, I've just gone paleo this year, and I feel amazing!"

"Paley-what?" Miles whispered to Laney.

"Good to see your excitement, Kate."

Holding palms out to the group, Glen said, "Okay. Just what does wellness include, and why does it matter to presence?"

"Fitness!"

"Nutrition?"

"Sleep, for sure. That's the extent of my wellness." Laney elbowed Miles.

"Anything else?" Glen asked.

"What about psychological health?"

Tom was interested in going deeper. "I could also see spiritual health and even emotional and mental health as fitting into the wellness category."

WELLNESS RADIATES HEALTH AND STAMINA AND PORTRAYS A LEVEL OF ENERGY THAT ATTESTS TO YOUR CAPABILITIES OF HANDLING THE HEAVY DEMANDS OF LEADERSHIP.

"I like how you're thinking outside the obvious," Glen agreed. "Yes, wellness includes more than your physical condition. It considers all of you—total body-mind-soul connection. Wellness radiates health and stamina and portrays a level of energy that attests to your capabilities of handling the heavy demands of leadership."

"Able-bodied leaders look the part." Jack's voice sounded from the back. He was standing now with arms crossed.

"Totally!" Kate was unnerved, the reality of standing in a minefield lost on her.

Glen swiftly directed the conversation to the board. "Take a look at these elements."

He wrote six words in a column: *exercise, nutrition, hydration, sleep, solitude,* and *recreation.*

"I'd like you to take a few minutes to reflect upon these elements of wellness as they pertain to your life. What is going well, and what would you like to change?"

"Hold the bus. What does solitude have to do with wellness?" Maryann asked.

"Would anyone care to speak to Maryann's question?" Glen responded.

"I will." Sondra directed her full gaze at Maryann. "Solitude helps us reconnect with ourselves and detox from influences that bombard us continually as leaders."

"I know all about the need for silence, but what about a person with a schedule like mine..."

Sondra interjected. "He said solitude, not silence. There's a difference. Solitude is about choosing to be by yourself—purposely finding space away from others. Silence is about quieting the noise, internal or external. You can actually experience silence even in a group. But solitude requires aloneness."

Everyone watched the real Sondra emerge.

Maryann stared blankly.

Glen waited ten seconds before responding.

"Thank you, Sondra, for sharing the difference. Please spend the next ten minutes or so reflecting upon your own wellness as addressed in these elements. Better yet, find some solitude in which to reflect. Feel free to go in the hallway, the café, a vacant room to be by yourself— anywhere but your office, where you'll be tempted to address issues that have crept up or sneak a peek at your e-mail. You need and deserve this time of quiet. So report back at eleven thirty. By then, it'll be time for us to move into the second layer."

Glen watched them trickle out one by one, reflecting.

Jack, too, moved out of the room, empty-handed. Except for his phone.

6

MANNERS MATTER

"Who's hungry?" Glen asked.

Everyone but Jack had made it back to the conference room by eleven thirty. He waited until their side conversations lessened a bit before starting again. Glen was certain they looked more relaxed than before.

"So I have a proposition to make." He stood before them, hands clasped together. "We've touched upon the key ideas from the outermost layer of leadership presence—style. A hefty external layer, eh? Almost three hours' worth."

That brought a round of guffaws.

"I propose we begin the second layer, etiquette, here and then continue our discussion at lunch. A working lunch, you might say. Shall we?"

"Game on!"

"I'm in."

"Me too." A cacophony of yeses.

"You're such an agreeable bunch."

Glen reached for a dry erase marker and headed toward the whiteboard. He drafted some phrases.

"A quick recap," he said as he wrote. "One, we talked already about the fact you're visible as a leader—always. Second, we've also touched upon the reality that people form first impressions of you within seconds or, rather, in fractions of a second. And third, we even discussed that you can largely influence others' perceptions of you by adjusting your behaviors."

1. You are visible.
2. People form impressions of you.
3. Adjust your behavior to influence perceptions.

As he turned back to the group, he said, "Bottom line, then, the quality of your leadership presence depends on your development of five skill sets that work collectively to portray you and what you represent. Does that sound accurate?"

He watched them nod as they transferred his words to their notepads. He returned the marker to its tray and headed to the back of the room to observe them.

"Let's say you've made a good first impression on someone checking you out as a leader," Glen proposed. "Most likely, the observer spends the rest of the conversation—or, at least, the next several encounters with you—confirming the initial impression. So the way you handle yourself when interacting with others can influence a longer-lasting judgment. That's where etiquette comes in. I like to think of it as social protocol or conventional grace."

Laney sat up straight. "Oh, I like the sound of that. My cousin attended an etiquette training school in D.C. when she was young, and I've always admired the way she handles herself in social settings. She stands out while still putting everyone else at ease. It's really amazing, actually."

"You bet, Laney. Etiquette implies thoughtful attention to small behaviors that increase others' comfort level with you. These nuanced moves help you to smoothly navigate social dynamics."

Kate quickly finished scrawling her notes and looked up. "I'm so glad we're going to do this! If I could figure out how to act smooth and elegant, oh, wow, that would be something. I would feel confident."

Sondra watched the conversation, puzzled. "Glen, could you clarify something for me?"

"Gladly."

"Is etiquette the same as elegance?"

He tipped his head back and thought deeply for a few seconds. "Elegance could be a result of etiquette, but etiquette's goal is not to just promote elegance. A better way to look at it is to think of etiquette as polish—polish that helps us connect hospitably with others. Let me break it down into its parts so you can see what it contains."

Glen went back to the board and wrote *etiquette* with four bullets underneath it: *manners, dining, networking,* and *e-professionalism.*"

Etiquette
- Manners
- Dining
- Networking
- E-professionalism

"Aha! That's why you're taking us out to lunch," Miles said.

"Nice catch, Miles."

He transitioned again. "Please stand up and find someone you haven't talked much with today. Look each other in the eye, shake hands, and find a comfortable place to sit, facing each other."

The room came alive with movement.

~

What is the secret to rapport? Meet people where they are. That's what Glen did.

"If you haven't already, turn your chairs to face one another. Thank you. All right, nice. We have Miles and Tom, Laney and Kate, and Maryann and Sondra. Now, please close your eyes and tell yourself that the person sitting in front of you is important."

Glen walked amid the pairs, watching their reactions.

"I know this seems weird, Maryann. Just go with me on this." Sondra nudged her into a small smile.

After ten somewhat awkward seconds, Glen broke the silence. "Tom, why would I have you do that before we start our conversation on manners?"

"Well, I suppose you want us to get into the habit of really seeing the person before us, you know, making sure the other person knows he matters."

"Can I add a thought?"

Glen motioned for Sondra to continue. "When you're kind and courteous to everyone you meet, you stand out as someone who cares. And people remember that! Everyone's in a rush, and that leads to rudeness. And there's a lot of rudeness. It's refreshing and far too rare to bump into someone who's considerate."

Sondra didn't intend to look Maryann's way; it just happened. She'd become engrossed in what she was saying. It wasn't until Maryann's lips tightened into a grimace that it dawned on her how directional the comment might have sounded.

No one else said a word.

But, wait. Wasn't that a good thing, Sondra thought? Didn't Maryann need to realize how she came across to almost everyone?

Sondra battled with herself for what felt like an eternity until Maryann spoke.

"I've been told I come across as rude."

Sondra listened in quiet, while everyone stared at Maryann.

"I'm only being real. It's hard to fake feeling cheery." She sounded defensive and, yet, strangely sad. Sondra's heart melted a little for Maryann. Perhaps there was a back story.

Kate beat her to the punch. "I know what you mean, Maryann. I have to deal with a hundred different things at the same time at my desk too. And sometimes I feel like hitting the next person who comes in to interrupt me."

Laney spit out a laugh.

Kate continued. "Okay. That was a little random. Sorry. What I'm trying to say is that using good manners with people isn't easy. But it's important. I think your job is like mine in that we greet people who come into an office. Right, Maryann?"

"Yes."

"Yeah. Then it's doubly important for us."

She leaned in to look Maryann in the eye. Gradually, Maryann transferred her gaze from the floor to Kate's face. She gave a short, tight nod.

Glen inserted himself into the conversation to lighten the mood.

"Pairs, I'm passing around a list with some common tips for developing good manners. I'd like you to practice using these manners with one another, but we'll walk through them as a group. You can use the instruction sheet to assist you."

After some fidgeting, the pairs settled down to begin.

"Tip number one is smile," Glen directed. "Lift those cheeks and eyebrows. Give each other a genuine smile. Research proves a real smile can actually boost your mood."

Their smiles ranged from goofy to cheeky to heartfelt.

"How does that make you feel to receive a hearty smile?" Glen asked.

"When Miles smiled at me for real," Tom said, "I felt noticed and valued."

SMILE. SAY THANK YOU. GREET OTHERS BY THEIR NAME.

"Ah gee, thanks, Tom."

"Continue the smiles, but let's add tip number two, offer common courtesies. As you can see on your sheet, that means such phrases as 'please' and 'thank you' and 'pardon me.' Practice them a bit in imaginary conversation, and then tell me what effect they have."

Glen filtered through the group, observing their comic interactions. Laney was the first to respond. "As I'm experimenting with Kate, I'm thinking that I probably notice these phrases more when they're *not* said."

"Yeah, I totally take them for granted. But boy, do I sure dislike a lack of courtesy!" Kate said.

Comfortable with the camaraderie building, Tom threw out another question. "What do you all think about courtesy in writing—you know, like e-mail or notes?"

"Personally, I am greatly touched when I receive a handwritten thank-you note or a sympathy card," Sondra said.

"Would you share your thinking on that, Sondra?"

"Well, it means someone has gone the extra mile to say he or she cares."

"Agreed," Glen said. "It seems to me that a lot of people fail to respond to my e-mails after I've answered a question or given them information. It's like they have what they need, so good-bye, good riddance. Does anyone else have that problem?" Several began talking at once.

Glen continued. "In the most polite way possible, I'm going to interrupt the conversation and turn your attention to tip number three, greet others by name, because it speaks to the point Tom's raising. Talk to one another for a few minutes, being sure to use your names in dialogue. Pay attention to what you notice."

He waited a few minutes before cutting in on them. "What did you notice?"

Maryann cautiously offered her opinion. "I guess in a little way, it helped me not be so self-absorbed. I had to focus on someone else other than myself or my tasks."

"You bet. Making a point to greet those who cross your path—a matter of seconds—helps affirm your presence in two beneficial ways. First, for others, it offers a moment of recognition. People who are 'seen' feel validated. Second, for you, it reinforces your determination to respect others' existence as unique individuals. Kind of what Tom was getting at when he asked about people's failure to respond."

"Like living in the present moment, right?" Kate asked.

"Exactly. Thanks, Kate."

"Moving on. Tip number four is practice deference and use titles. That's not something we need to practice, per se. But know that if someone you're addressing has a title—such as president or doctor or reverend—use it unless they direct it otherwise. The same goes for people you are meeting formally for the first time. Use Mr., Mrs., or Ms. for those you don't know until you are on a first-name basis."

Laney flagged her hand. "I'm not disagreeing with you, Glen. But isn't that a little too uptight? I don't know that anyone has ever called me Ms. Richards."

"Well, just because something's common doesn't mean it's the best way. A good rule of thumb is to demonstrate conventional or expected etiquette to show you do know good manners. Treat others respectfully by dignifying their name and title. You can always adjust based on the information you gather about them or what's expected. Remember, as a leader, you want to be more concerned about the other person than yourself."

"Hmm. I've never thought about it quite like that before," admitted Laney.

It was turning out to be an enlightening day after all.

~

"Stand up, everyone! Time to get the blood flowing."

Glen trotted back and forth among the pairs, gesturing for them to get up and out of their seats. Miles and Kate hopped up quickly, eager to move. Tom and Laney were slower to rise, and Maryann reluctantly forced herself to stand, smoothing out her gray pants as she stood. She showed less resistance than before.

"I'd like you to form two lines, facing one another. We're going to practice tip number five, which is extending a handshake, so make sure someone else is directly across from you in line."

He stood back and watched the group assemble. "Be sure to face someone other than your partner."

The chatter quickly turned away from the focus of manners. Glen reined them back in.

"On the count of three, walk toward your partner, introduce yourself, and shake hands. No pressure here. Just do what you normally do."

Voices and hands mingled. Glen saw plenty to address.

"Freeze!" All motion ceased, except for a few nervous giggles.

"Stay right where you are. But turn your eyes to Tom." Tom reddened at the thought of others staring at him; he'd never liked being in the spotlight.

"What message does Tom's handshake send?"

"It's weak. That's what." No one had expected Jack to enter at that moment. Even Glen had forgotten about him.

He headed off the collision. "Jack, this question is for the group, not observers."

Jack shook off the correction with a shrug of his shoulders and sauntered toward the back wall near the windows.

Sondra, who was receiving Tom's handshake, said, "Tom, if you could squeeze my hand a little more, and add a shake or two, you'd be demonstrating your confidence in me and in yourself."

Tom's eyes thanked her for saving face.

"Kate, what suggestions would you offer Miles?" Glen asked.

"Not so tight." She squealed in fake pain. Miles glanced at his hand cupping Kate's, her fingers red on the tips.

"Sorry! My bad, Kate!"

His apology brought a welcome relief of laughter.

"Maryann? What feedback would you offer Laney?"

"Well, for starters, holding my hand like that creeps me out. I don't know you very well, and it's weird to think you want to double-clasp my hand. And back up!"

Laney dropped one hand to her side, surprised more than hurt. "I'd always thought that was a sophisticated handshake. I see politicians do it all the time." She sought Glen for support.

"Yes, it can be appropriate, Laney, when the occasion fits. It can be used when showing deep respect or fondness for someone you know well. But I'd caution against using it as your regular, signature handshake, after all, when people first meet you."

"Especially with people who want extra personal space." Maryann followed up her words with a smug smile—an afterthought.

"Maryann brings up a valid point," Glen said. "Personal space is huge. Everyone has a different appreciation for what's comfortable, but in general, less than two feet away is reserved for intimate relationships with family or friends. Business conversations should generally be kept within the four- to twelve-foot range, depending upon whether they are small-group or large-group discussions."

"So what about hugging then?" Kate asked with her hands on her hips. "I sure see lots of hugs in the gathering space off the elevators and by the front entrance."

"Perfect timing for tip number six, which is hug with caution. The big thing to remember with hugging—besides being aware of personal space—is to read the other person's body language. If your company culture supports hugging, if the other person initiates it or is open to receiving a hug, and if you're not crossing any boundaries (like hugging someone else's wife or hugging your superior), then a brief hug can be acceptable. Hug and release. Don't linger or sway."

"No doubt. That's hokey," said Miles.

Glen smiled. "Yes, Miles. And respect the fact that some people do not want to be hugged. If in doubt, just… don't," pretending to slice his throat. "Got it?"

"Yes, sir!"

"Great. Why don't you move on back to your seats? We can touch upon the last three manners quickly."

~

After the bustling settled down, Glen announced tip number seven, arriving promptly. He shared that being fashionably late might be acceptable for a formal gala, but keeping others waiting for you in professional settings is disrespectful; it shows a lack of concern for another's valuable time. Rather, he said, strive to be early for all meetings and appointments. This way, you will be present—literally—in plenty of time to acclimate yourself to the environment and prepare to give the best of yourself.

"If you end up being late by accident, notify the one who's waiting. E-mail, call, text. Somehow, let the person know why and when you're planning to arrive. So much of good manners comes down to being considerate," Glen said.

Miles sat back in his chair, taking it all in. "This stuff seems so commonsense. I mean, what's the point?"

"What's the point of what, this training?" Glen asked.

"Yeah."

Glen glanced at the group thoughtfully, as if he were hiding something from them.

"Executing good manners makes good sense. But that doesn't mean everyone shows good manners," he said. "Jack invited me to this office to offer my thoughts on how to improve the leadership. After observing for over a week, it became clear that strengthening leadership presence would address a number of the issues. Or, at the very least, put necessary elements into order so critical issues could be more easily fixed. Using good manners is one piece of one layer of presence."

Glen paused before delivering the news. "And I can assure you that no one here consistently exercises good manners. May I give you an example?"

"All right." Miles dragged out his skepticism.

"Tip number eight is don't interrupt. Since we began this morning, I have witnessed almost everyone interrupt someone."

"Except me." Again, Jack's voice came out of nowhere.

"Actually, that includes you too, Jack."

"When?"

Glen walked toward Jack, pointing to his hand.

"Your cell phone. It's a constant source of interruption. While you sit in the back of the room, set apart from the group, you stay engrossed in your phone, and that is inconsiderate of our time and presence. We can tell when your attention is divided when you've put us on hold."

He left Jack open-mouthed and directed his attention toward the group. "Without making a conscientious point to listen actively to what another is saying, time and time again, you can easily fall into the habit of interrupting. And this habit is offensive."

He could tell their memories were thinking through the morning's conversations. "If you do realize you've interrupted someone, it's best to acknowledge and apologize. And make every effort not to do it again!"

Despite thick tension in the room, Glen decided to proceed with the final tip.

"Tip number nine is simple but powerful: watch your words. Plainly stated, profane, vulgar, disrespectful, or derogatory language has no place in business communication. You could offend someone, first of all, and it cheapens your credibility."

"So," Tom said, "you're basically telling us that to be well-mannered, we must always be courteous and clean."

"Yes, a good summation, Tom."

They had taken the information better than he expected. Glen knew real change took time and personal accountability, but his part of the endeavor was coming along nicely.

No sense in losing steam.

"Didn't I promise you lunch?" Glen asked.

7

STICK A FORK IN IT
(AND A KNIFE)

They packed themselves tightly into the company SUV.

Everyone but Jack. He chose to use the guest office space to catch up on work. He couldn't afford to waste time, he said.

Glen estimated they were slightly behind schedule. He'd better creatively make up time during the meal. They hadn't even begun digging into the deep stuff.

He maneuvered the Merton Financial Yukon out of the parking lot as he explained the importance of the dining experience to etiquette. Because so many business transactions occur during meals, a leader with presence should master social conventions as both a host and a guest.

Kate proclaimed her glee from the third-row passenger seat. "Oh, I love to host parties!"

Glen caught her eye in the rearview mirror. "Would you be willing to share some tips you've learned hosting?"

"Gladly."

Kate scooched forward in her seat, crowding into Tom's space. She proceeded to explain the importance of making guests feel welcome and comfortable. How it's best to get to know the guests' interests before they arrive, if possible, and to definitely think through logistical procedures.

She jabbered on. "You know, where everyone will sit, how the food will be laid out, the order of events. Stuff like that."

Glen waited for her to take a breath before inserting a comment. "Thank you, Kate. I would also add that, as host, you are responsible for financing the meal and setting the mood. So organizing and delegating the menu, drink selection, decoration, food preparation, and service all fall within your domain."

Kate picked up the baton and ran. "For sure! I like to envision how I want the event to unfold—you know, like, play it out in my mind. Who is going to be there? What is the purpose of the event? What do I want to achieve through this gathering? That kind of thing."

"So being artfully attentive, right?" Laney admired her own cleverness.

"Yes, Laney. Preparing and serving, simply."

Glen turned into DeLiano's Bistro. The parking lot was jam-packed.

They piled out of the SUV, happy for the freedom to stretch.

"You mentioned this would be a working lunch, Glen. What exactly are we going to be doing?"

Glen grinned at Miles and made a forward motion with his hands to direct everyone toward the front door. "You'll see."

~

Luigi DeLiano greeted them with a warm, boisterous welcome. He had reserved a special room in the back for their business luncheon. Obviously, he had insider information.

DeLiano's was a Seattle favorite. The delicious smells and authentic Italian ambience put everyone at ease. Glen's spirit soared.

Each place setting had a large dinner plate, three glasses (two for wine and one for water), two spoons, a knife, three forks, a bread and butter plate, a butter knife, and a napkin. Sitting atop the large dinner plate was a small laminated picture of a formal place setting and a name card.

"Please, find your name." Glen stood at the head of the table, patiently waiting. Once all were seated, he remained standing.

"As you know, we're working through the second layer of leadership presence: etiquette. We've talked about exercising good manners, and we know we're going to focus on dining etiquette. Consider it an honor when you're invited to a dinner meeting or event. Your behavior before, during, and after the meal should reflect your recognition of the meal's importance. With that, please stand back up."

Chairs pushed back until everyone was standing awkwardly. "Of course, etiquette protocol will vary

depending upon how well you know the host, but when you're the guest, it is customary to shake hands with all seated at the table and to remain standing until the host sits. Shall we practice?"

Knowing this was more of a command than a question, Sondra turned to her right and extended a hand to Maryann.

"Hello! My name is Sondra Pfeiffer from Merton Financial. What is your name?"

Maryann extended her hand and proceeded to introduce herself. Others in the group followed suit until soon the room was filled with conversational chatter. Glen then made an exaggerated show of sitting down, motioning for all to join him.

"This portion of the training will consist of show and tell." The group chuckled.

Glen said, "I'd like to offer a few tips before we order off the menu. Be sure to sit up straight. Good posture signals confidence. Also, when our waiter comes, don't ask him to explain every item on the menu. Seriously! I've seen people do that."

Glen coached the group to take the host's lead in ordering, especially alcoholic beverages, and to avoid sloppy or hard-to-eat foods. He warned them not to order the most expensive item on the menu and to keep the conversation light—nothing too personal or controversial.

Ordering went without a hitch. They sipped coffee and sparkling water until the waiter brought out their meals. Those who had salads with their meals were instructed to begin with the outermost fork; the next in would be for the main meal.

After everyone had been served, Glen held out two hands, palms out, to halt them. "Capture this visual in your mind. Solids foods are on your left. Bread, for example. And drinks are on your right. Your water glass sits closest to your plate."

He went on to explain how to cut their meat one piece at a time (and butter bread one bite at a time) and to lay the knife across the plate between cuts. Don't grip the utensils. Hold the knife or fork with the thumb and three fingers, keeping the index finger extended on the handle.

Instructions continued throughout the course of the meal. Keep your elbows off the table. Don't double-dip. Don't speak with your mouth full. When you speak, put your silverware on your plate, not on the table. Don't reach; ask someone to pass whatever it is you want. Maintain good eye contact with each person at the table, and take your time eating, talking, and listening to everyone at the table.

They chuckled about not eating off another person's plate or licking their fingers or silverware or overindulging. They made a point to say extra "pleases" and "thank yous," especially to the servers. And when Miles accidentally dropped his knife on the floor, Glen stopped him midaction from picking it up.

As they finished eating, Glen showed them how to politely wipe the edges of their mouths with a napkin. He placed his napkin to the left of his plate, signaling the end of the meal and explained that if they needed to leave the table, they should place their napkin on their seat rather than on the table, to show they would be coming back. Each of them placed knife and fork prong-side up, side-by-side on the plate with handles at four o'clock and talked about how much they enjoyed the meal.

Glen collected the check when it arrived and explained that the proper response was gratitude for the meal rather than arguing to pay.

"The host who invited you must take care of both the check and the tip. And if we were leaving now, I would have you shake one another's hands again and avoid using toothpicks in front of others," he said.

They laughed at the randomness of his final words.

"But while we're here in this pleasant atmosphere, let's begin discussing the next aspect of etiquette. Anyone want to take a guess?"

The group members looked around at one another, clueless. He waited ten full seconds before responding.

"Networking."

Sondra, puzzled, spoke up. "Doesn't networking lead us in a different direction from what etiquette is supposed to do—show consideration and concern for others?"

"Not if it's done the right way."

"And we have no doubt, Glen, that you'll show us the right way!" Laney's jab left a twinkle in her eye.

"You know me well already."

He leaned forward, in his element.

～

Glen signaled Luigi over to their table.

Luigi picked up the signal and strode toward Glen, sharp in a gray pinstriped suit. In his strong carriage and pleasant demeanor, he embodied the distinction his grandfather infused into the Bistro two generations prior. People liked being near Luigi.

With a rich, throaty voice, he asked, hands open, "Mr. O'Brien, what can I get for you and your guests?" He then crossed his wrists at his waist, waiting to serve.

Glen faced Luigi. "Nothing more to eat or drink, Luigi! The meal was excellent, as always. But I would like you to share some of your wisdom with us."

Luigi's face radiated a quiet confidence. "Whatever I can do for you, sir," he nodded graciously.

"Luigi, please call me Glen."

"Of course, of course. My pleasure, Glen."

The party members attentively watched the polite interaction between two friendly acquaintances.

"Luigi, you are a highly respected leader in our Seattle community. You've managed to successfully carry on the traditions of your father and grandfather, and your business is stronger than ever."

Luigi's good-natured expression revealed his full interest in Glen.

"How have you used networking to strengthen your business and your presence as a leader?"

Luigi thought for a moment and then asked a simple question. "May I join you?"

So taken by his cordiality, the group quickly shuffled their chairs to make room for Luigi. Miles was the first to point out the available space between him and Glen.

Luigi pulled a side chair over and sat down, thanking Miles and the others.

"Uh, let me think." He rested for a few seconds.

In a soft Italian accent, he shared his heart.

"I have enjoyed many successes in my career because of the support and goodness of other people. My father taught me what his father taught him—to form healthy relationships with people who will help me get better. I can only do so much on my own, you know?" His eyes danced.

"Is that what you would say networking is?" Glen asked.

"Yes, yes. Networking is seeing and connecting together. As a leader, I must be what they call a talent seeker. Such an American word, no?" The group laughed along with him.

"Yes, yes, so I seek talent—in potential chefs, servers, hosts, and hostesses, and then I match it up with needs. And sometimes the talent and needs are my own and sometimes not."

Laney spoke up, intrigued. "I've always thought networking was a socially acceptable form of self-promotion. But you seem to have a different perspective, Luigi."

"Oh yes, it's more, much more." Luigi grew animated.

"But of course, I suppose some business people use or manipulate others as a way of growing in power, but that is not leadership. Real networking is about treating people well."

Glen looked around the table at the faces fixed on Luigi. They continued their conversation a few minutes longer before a young server came over to get Luigi. A patron was waiting to see him.

He stood. "Thank you, thank you for coming today to the Bistro! You are welcome as family here anytime," he extolled before taking his leave. They extended their sincere appreciation and well wishes with smiles and good-byes, touched by his kindness.

Laney waited a second for good measure before firing off the questions. "Glen, I need you to help me understand networking better. Where does it begin? I mean, how does a person *seek* talent? Specifics would help. No offense to anybody here, but I've been working with the same people for a while now. Wouldn't I already know who can do what?"

Sondra responded. "Based on what we've already learned today, it seems to me that networking is a highly sophisticated form of etiquette. Like it's a way to build strong relationships and engage in meaningful encounters with people where everyone benefits. Glen?"

"That's a nice way to describe networking, Sondra. Let's face it. Leaders are highly visible. They're purposefully visible. And they're also relational. They realize their work is done with and through people. Fostering supportive connections parallels professional success." They returned puzzled looks.

Miles boldly asked what all of them were thinking. "Then how has Jack become so successful?"

Glen tiptoed around the issue they wanted to spear.

"Jack's a master at strategic networking. He surrounds himself with centers of influence who put him in contact with others who can magnify his marketability. We can all learn a lot from Jack about how he navigates connections."

"But?" It was Miles, still questioning.

LEADERS ARE PURPOSEFULLY VISIBLE AND RELATIONAL. THEIR WORK IS DONE WITH AND THROUGH PEOPLE. FOSTERING SUPPORTIVE CONNECTIONS PARALLELS PROFESSIONAL SUCCESS.

"But the quality of Luigi's relationships with his customers, with his employees, with his family—lovely, by the way—is a testament to the soundness of his wisdom."

Glen stopped to weigh his words. "Whether you're seeking to grow your personal network, your workplace network, or your centers of influence, you can gain solid ground by approaching these relationships from the perspective of someone seeking to develop talent and meet needs."

"True colors shine forth over time." Tom spoke to himself.

Everyone sat still thinking about what had transpired. Finally, Glen checked his watch.

"It's close to one thirty, and we have a rather full afternoon." He took a second to reorder priorities.

"We have one last component of etiquette to discuss on the ride back. Is everyone okay with that?"

"Do we have a choice?"

"Actually, no, Miles. But thanks for asking."

They were down to less than a day and a half.

And still so much work remained.

⁓

Maryann was first to reach the SUV.

She'd been ready to leave an hour earlier. Her age bore down upon her. Maybe it was all the talking doing her in. All this bothersome talk. So much talking.

She stood by the locked Yukon while Glen fidgeted for his keys. Why couldn't everyone just leave her alone? Her flight back to Chicago wasn't until tomorrow evening, with Jack. He insisted they fly first-class together. She couldn't even have peace there—in the air, the flight attendant checking in every fifteen minutes and Jack flitting between self-absorbed small talk and brooding silence. She sighed out loud, remembering yesterday's painful flight to Seattle. She really couldn't say how or why she'd put up with him for so many years.

"Are you okay, Maryann?" Kate's concern was genuine.

Where to begin with this naïve child, thought Maryann. "I'm fine."

Her sourness was an unfair but involuntary response. She'd learned it was easier to put people off than shut them up.

Maryann opened the handle after hearing Glen hit the unlock button and stepped into the driver's side backseat. Out of sight, out of mind, she hoped.

But Tom squeezed in right beside her, still smelling of strong aftershave.

"Hello."

She'd never cared for fragile Tom and had not figured out why Jack held on to someone so spineless for nearly a year.

She faked an interested smile and then turned toward the window, sighing.

Glen caught Miles before he slid into the front passenger seat. "Care to drive, Miles?"

"Sure. I'm game." Miles grabbed the keys from Glen and situated himself in the driver's seat. He faced the group squished like sardines in a can and said cheerily, "Buckle up. Anyone need some gum?"

"Me." Kate was the lone taker.

Glen took Miles's spot and trumpeted to no one in particular, "Home, James," as the SUV veered out of the still-busy parking lot. Once they hit the main street headed back to the office, Glen directed the conversation back to etiquette.

"We have one more aspect to discuss: e-professionalism," Glen began, as he turned to address the sardines. "Due to networking and global business practices, leaders are inundated with communication requests via multiple technological mediums. Much good comes to organizations and their clients through social media. But we'd be foolish to not address the behavioral expectations when using social media. Behaving appropriately online, in a way that satisfies expected customs, has become known as e-professionalism."

"Say what you just said in a nutshell," Miles challenged Glen.

"Gladly," Glen said. "Be careful of what you put out there on the Internet for others to see. It affects your presence."

"That's pretty commonsense," said Kate.

"I'm not so sure. Tons of people think it's perfectly acceptable to share highly personal pictures of themselves," Laney added.

Miles dug in further. "What's the problem with that? They're just being real."

"She's saying that too often lines become blurred." Sondra looked back at Miles. "I mean, do our clients need to know what parties you attended over the weekend?"

For a split second, Sondra regretted not using her filter.

"Gee whiz, Sondra. Get off my case. What are you doing, spying on me?"

"You know I don't spy, Miles. I heard about your wild party from someone else in the office. Word spreads quickly. I should have said something to you right away."

Miles reddened. "Sounds like there's a lot you don't tell us we should know!"

His words stung. Sondra's eyes welled with tears. She faced straight ahead, neck stiffened.

Glen intervened. "Look at the big picture, folks. No one's going to ding anyone else. The point I'm making in regard to e-professionalism is that everything you say about yourself and others will be open for interpretation, so be careful, thoughtful, and ethical about what you write, which sites you frequent, and how you present yourself online. Any information you share through social media could be accessed by anyone, anywhere."

"I know some of our more tech savvy employees are using Facebook and Twitter for social interaction. And most of them are younger," Sondra said. "I'm just wondering if we need some guidance on what to tell them. In a hiring situation, I don't search prospective employees on social media, but some of my HR colleagues do. They tell me it's not pretty to see a potential hire talking about getting drunk at a class reunion."

"Sondra, you're right on the money," Glen said. "Seriously though, I challenge each of you to spend the remaining minutes thinking quietly about your social media activity—how you present yourself as an online user in your personal and professional lives. What might others think about you based on what you share?"

"I don't use social media," Maryann said.

Glen resisted the urge to roll his eyes. "That's fine, Maryann. Then spend the rest of the trip back in silence."

Jack was not paying him enough for this favor.

~

Glen hated feeling snarky.

He locked the Yukon and trekked across the dimly lit parking garage to the level one entrance. He took brisk steps to work out frustration that had seeped in over the morning. The hardest part was yet to come.

He entered the lobby and found the group milling near the front counter that also served as Kate's desk. She was showing Maryann something on her computer. Tom and Miles were engrossed in their phones, oblivious to Laney, who was lapping the perimeter of the lobby.

Where had Sondra gone? She needed the next session more than any of the others.

Kate spotted Glen first. "We're ready when you are, Glen!"

She closed up the program before Maryann was ready. Glen called the others, until everyone hovered around Kate's desk.

"Has anyone seen Sondra?"

"I'm here."

A small voice came from behind him. He turned to find she'd been crying.

"For a change, we're going to move the next session into the boardroom," Glen perked up his voice.

"Do you have permission?" Maryann spared no mercy. "No one is permitted in a Merton Financial boardroom without Jack's permission."

Glen returned her question with surprising zeal. "Yes, I do. In fact, Jack will be joining us in the boardroom."

Even a cattle prod couldn't have moved them along faster.

8

~

CAN YOU HEAR ME NOW?

Jack had designed all the Merton Financial boardrooms himself. But the Seattle branch's boardroom was his personal favorite. It resembled a movie theater with its sloping floor and stadium seating. Unlike the glass and marble prominent throughout the officeplex, the boardroom's soundproof walls, soft lighting, and plush carpet amplified sounds and directed visitors' attention to the front of the room, down the center.

A semicircular desk rested in the middle of a raised platform sitting at the end of the sloped floor. Seven leather conference chairs rimmed the outside of the curved, pristine desk. Jack sat propped up in the middle chair, the shiny, black soles of his shoes perched on top of the desk. The glaring spotlights above bore down on his face; he appeared almost cruel.

Glen swore he had entered an interrogation room.

Sondra, right behind Glen, was the first in the group to notice Jack. She lost her breath for a second, the others filing in behind her.

"What?"

Irritated by the hold up, Maryann pushed her way through Sondra and Tom, both frozen. As her eyes adjusted to the dark, the view below became clear. She gasped and put her hands on her hips.

"Jack Merton! What on earth are you doing? Stop looking pathetic." Maryann stormed down the aisle.

"The rest of us have been stuck together—*forced* together by *you*, and you've been hiding out here playing make-believe." She ranted, waggling a stern finger.

Maryann's relationship with Jack was one of tolerance. She had put up with him for twenty-some years because she had to. She had zero respect for the man. She'd lost hope years ago that things would get better. Now she was biding her time.

But the day's stress had taken its toll. And Maryann snapped.

Jack yanked his feet off the desk and shot up straight and tall, adjusting his suit jacket and smoothing his hair. He braced himself to face her fury.

Glen, hot on her tail, thrust himself between them.

"Jack, glad to see you back." He bounded up onto the stage and faced a cold Jack, nose to nose.

"I don't know where you've been, but your presence is required from here on out." Glen's stance, arms on his hips, showed his intent.

Bristling, Jack's eyes turned from Glen to an expectant Maryann at the end of the center aisle, then back to Glen.

"Remember our deal?" Glen reminded Jack. "I lead. The problems here in Seattle will remain until you're here to see—and own them." He was not willing to budge.

"This better be good, O'Brien."

Glen set a cold stare until Jack buckled.

Then he turned back to the group.

"Come on down, everyone. We're ready to get started with the third layer of leadership presence."

The rest of the group crept forward with caution.

"Keep coming. All the way down to the front of the raised platform."

As they assembled, Glen busied himself with technology. Soon, a large, white screen emerged from the ceiling behind the curved desk.

"Where do you want us to sit, Glen?" Kate infused her voice with sweet cheer.

"Yes, yes, anywhere in the front."

They filed into the first two rows right in front of the platform. Jack sat at least ten rows back from them.

A large graphic appeared on the screen before them.

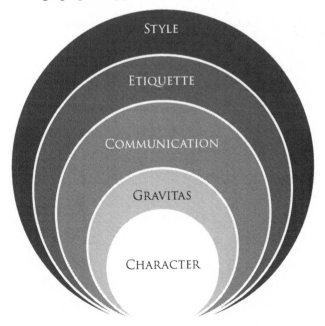

"Okay. So far, we've talked about the nature and purpose of leadership presence and the first two layers—style and etiquette." Glen's heartrate had slowed.

He determined to focus his energy on those he was being paid to help.

"What were some of the components of the first two layers?"

Laney spoke up. "I got this. I took notes."

A few chuckles sprang up. "First was presence, in general—like what it is and stuff. Then grooming. Then dress. That was a doozy! Then environment. Then wellness. All of that made up style. Then we moved on to etiquette. And that contained a bunch too. Manners, dining, networking, and e-professionalism." She double-checked her notes. "I think that's it, right?"

"Look at you go!" Kate let out a woohoo.

Building upon the lightheartedness, Glen pushed on. "Now, we're going to spend some time on the third layer, effective communication."

"Piece of cake!"

"Say again, Miles?"

"I double-majored in marketing and communication. I could practically teach this next session."

Glen harnessed his doubt. "Miles, would you please walk us through this communication model?"

Jack groaned. Glen darted a quick glare and then turned his attention toward Miles.

Miles oblivious to the overt disrespect, bounced up, happy for the opportunity to show what he knew. He first spoke about the sender who conceives an idea to be shared. How the sender determines the point to be expressed, the person or persons who will receive the idea, how the idea should be presented, and which medium to use for delivery.

Sondra leaned toward Laney and whispered, "I haven't seen him this animated in a long time." Laney smiled and nodded in agreement.

Glen added that much is weighed in this early decision-making process. The sender has to ask him or herself a series of questions (even if in milliseconds). What is the purpose? What is the intent? What are the receiver's needs? In what order should the ideas be developed? What language should be used? How might the receiver perceive what has been expressed? What concerns or biases might the receiver have? How can obstacles to interpretation be prevented? Why select this medium over that?

"Right," said Miles. "After making these choices, the sender encodes the message. That means he puts it in a deliverable form and sends it onward."

Miles continued with his explanation. He talked about the message's journey from sender to receiver—how it experiences "noise."

Kate had a few questions, so Miles explained that noise can be technical in nature: cyberspace pitfalls, technological delays, volume issues. Some noise can be structural such as grammar slips, incoherent thoughts, language confusion; and some noise is psychological: mood, tone, context, or mental and emotional stability.

"Then isn't it a miracle that good communication ever occurs?" Laney asked what several others were thinking.

"Precisely why we want to master some specific behaviors to enhance our effectiveness as communicators, especially when we're leading others," said Glen. "Miles, continue, please."

Miles then talked about the message finally reaching the receiver. Another series of questions occurs as the receiver accepts, decodes, interprets, and responds to the shared idea. The receiver with his or her own frame of reference seeks answers. What is being said? How? Why? What is the sender's intent? Why might this be? What should my response be? What is influencing my response? How should I respond? When? Why? What is my intention? What is my result?

He checked Glen's reaction for assurance. "You bet. The receiver then becomes the sender, and the cycle repeats."

Sondra had been listening, all ears. "Miles, how does feedback fit into the model?"

Miles sat on the edge of the raised platform, much more relaxed than when he began. For the first time all day, he felt he belonged. He crossed his sandaled feet at the ankles and swung them back and forth.

"Driving this process is feedback. Feedback is response information offered while the message is being delivered—orally—or after the message has been received, decoded, and interpreted. Kind of like what Glen just gave me."

Glen stepped forward. "You could say that feedback acts as a barometer, helping the sender gauge the success of the communication or identify ways to increase its effectiveness. Miles wanted to make sure he was on the right track—that I agreed, so he looked my way and scanned my expression to make that judgment call."

"Exactly," Miles affirmed. "It can fill in gaps and clarify understanding. Effective communicators pay attention to feedback—given and received—to increase the quality of message give-and-take."

Maryann was skeptical. "I'm not convinced it's possible to avoid misunderstanding," she said, crossing her arms.

Sondra spoke up, genuinely mindful of Maryann's concern. "Maryann, I'm not either, but I think Miles and Glen are explaining the communication model so that we can take proactive measures of preventing the potential for misunderstanding."

"Thank you, Sondra," Glen said.

He left the platform to pick up a poster-board easel resting against the back wall behind the curved desk. He lugged it onto the platform. Miles pulled himself up to help.

With the easel in place, Glen set to work drafting ideas. He talked out loud while he sketched.

"As Miles explained, communication begins with crafting a message to send. But I'd like to take us back one more step—into the mind of the sender."

"Oh boy, here we go." The impatient remark came from the back of the room. Jack had moved into the shadows near the double-doored entrance.

Ignoring Jack, Glen explained that message construction begins with your thinking or, more precisely, the fuel of your thoughts: your assumptions.

"Assumptions are conclusions you believe to be true," he said. "These could be conclusions about what others already know or value, why something is the way it is, or even the motive behind a certain action or response. For example, a client who enters the doors of the Merton Financial office in Seattle assumes that people who work at a financial company know how to balance their checkbooks."

This brought a couple of laughs. "And that they like math." More snickers. "And that they *want* to be there."

The silence lasted a few seconds until Tom spoke.

"Tell us more."

Glen proceeded. "Okay, so assumptions bleed into your thinking, almost to the point that you don't even notice the role they play in shaping your perspective— even if they're not accurate."

Laney raised her hand. "Wait a minute. Are you suggesting people are walking around with thoughts that might not be based on anything accurate?"

"Possibly, yes, or unfounded. This becomes problematic if the assumptions remain unchecked or buried, you might say. Use me as an example. I could look out at you all and assume you fully understand what I'm saying because I see Sondra nodding and Jack almost falling asleep. Now, that assumption may or may not be accurate, and the effectiveness of my actions because of my assumption will either improve or impair my communication with you."

Glen handed Miles some papers from his briefcase to distribute. "Bottom line, the purpose, manner, and style of your communication with others bear the imprint of the assumptions you have derived from their words and actions—and the assumptions they have made from yours."

He inserted a dramatic pause. "See? You are making assumptions of me right now too! Some of you may assume I know what I'm talking about, that I have credibility to back up my words. Others may be thinking I'm here with you in Seattle this week to earn some extra cash." He grinned. "Right or wrong, the assumptions you and others form heavily impact your attitudes and responses toward people and situations."

"But how do we know? This seems like something big—like I better get a handle on it," Kate said.

Kate's exasperation pierced Sondra's heart. She'd been pondering the same question.

Glen softened his voice. "You won't know the validity of your assumptions unless you make a point to check them—unless you willingly and honestly examine what has shaped your thinking and why. This takes courage."

> ASSUMPTIONS BLEED INTO YOUR THINKING, ALMOST TO THE POINT THAT YOU DON'T EVEN NOTICE THE ROLE THEY PLAY IN SHAPING YOUR PERSPECTIVE.

"May I offer a thought?" Tom asked.

"Of course, Tom. Please."

"Because we're talking about leadership presence, it seems pretty important that we look at assumptions as a way of becoming a better communicator in order to have stronger presence."

Tom looked down at the ground for a second and then adjusted his position to face the rest of the group in the front two rows. "I have to admit that I've never done a good job of examining my assumptions. My thinking has always been shallow. In fact, I haven't even assumed I've had assumptions. Am I making any sense?"

"Is that an apology?" came Jack's voice from the midway point of the audience.

"Well, I—"

"Because if it is, I'd like to hear it more clearly. I *assume* you mean it."

Sondra couldn't have predicted what happened next.

White, hot rage surged through every fiber of her being, igniting what must have been a torrent of flames. Ferocious waves of pure anger throttled out.

She tore out of her seat and lunged toward Jack.

"How dare you speak to him like that! *You* of all people. But I shouldn't be surprised. You don't have the human decency to consider your arrogance. Just what could this company be if its leader saw himself as he truly is?"

Tom held her arms back from thrashing. He bolted her to himself to keep her from hitting the ground, or Jack. Miles shielded his eyes, and Kate slunk low and scrambled across the floor to collect Sondra's belongings she'd flung away in the fit. Maryann was staring at Sondra as if she'd lost her mind. And Laney's face showed sympathy, the kind that says, "You probably shouldn't have said that, even if Jack deserved it."

Sondra knew she had crossed the line. With her anger spent, she hung her head and slowed her thrashing. Tom eased his grip and helped her calm down.

Somewhat unsure of what to do, Glen did nothing but wait in the tension of the moment.

He didn't have to wait long. Jack charged out of the room.

~

Maryann broke the silence.

She started clapping. Soon, Tom and Laney and Kate and Miles joined. A rush of serotonin quickly replaced the high levels of cortisol in her body, and Sondra dropped into her seat, shivering. Then the tears flowed. Years of pent-up frustration spilled out. The others gathered around her and just listened.

Glen slipped out undetected to grab some Kleenex.

Jack was nowhere to be seen. Everyone on the third floor was absorbed in their work, as if the incident hadn't occurred.

He ducked into the men's restroom to catch his breath and collect himself. He headed straight for the sink and splashed cool water on his face.

"I should have expected this kind of reaction to Jack," he said aloud. It wasn't a matter of *if* but *when*.

He washed again, thinking through the remaining plans for the day. Adjustments were in order. Think, think, think…

He dried his hands and face carefully and looked at his reflection one more time in the mirror.

Then it clicked.

Of course. He knew what needed to happen.

He smiled at himself.

Why hadn't he thought of this before? He'd just cooked up a game-changer.

~

Glen poked his head into the boardroom.

He planned to announce their next destination, but the view inside floored him. Sondra, Laney, Miles, Tom, Kate, and Maryann—all of them but Jack—sat clustered together, engaged in what looked like an intense conversation.

They spoke in hushed voices, nodding and gesturing, as if they shared profound interest in what each other was saying.

A transformation had occurred. He couldn't have orchestrated their unity better himself.

None of them heard Glen approach. But he heard snippets:

"What do you think we should do?"

"Maybe if we all confronted him together."

"Yeah, safety in numbers, right?"

"I don't know. We'd be risking a lot."

"For sure. What if it backfired?"

Glen slipped into the seat behind Maryann. "Sounds like a serious conversation."

Maryann jumped in her seat, then welcomed Glen. "Geez! You startled me."

All in sync again, Sondra brought Glen up to speed.

After Jack had stormed out, Maryann started clapping. Others joined in, and before she knew it, tears flowed. As the team members came together to comfort Sondra, something just happened. They sat down and began sharing frustrations and fears about the Seattle office. All their concerns somehow involved Jack.

"And all this transpired while I was getting Kleenex?"

"You were gone longer than you think." Laney toyed with him. "I guess conflict can bring people together."

"True. Better yet, I had an epiphany too—an idea for how we can capitalize on this team energy and allay some of your concerns about Jack."

Miles spoke for the group. "We're all ears."

~

Glen pitched the plan.

"We have the rest of the afternoon to learn about the communication layer of leadership presence, and we have all of tomorrow to focus on the last two layers— the deepest layers: gravitas and character. But as I've mentioned before, the layers interact with one another."

"The zero-entry swimming pool." Kate glanced at Maryann whose face shone bright in response.

"Right. So what if we used this afternoon's communication session and tomorrow's final two layers to wrap up our understanding of presence and then use what we've learned to prepare an intervention for Jack?"

Tom sat back, unsure. "An intervention, Glen? That's a serious step."

Glen let the comment sit for a few seconds. "What does the group think?" He read their intent faces.

"If it can be done professionally," Sondra said, "it seems necessary. Or I'm not sure things will ever change in our office."

"What is an intervention?" Kate asked.

Glen answered Kate's question with professional discretion. "An intervention is an organized attempt by a group of people to bring about change in someone's thoughts and behaviors. The group confronts a specific person in a nonthreatening way about a self-destructive problem—with the hope that the person will see what needs to change."

The silence grew awkward.

"Let me offer this option," Glen said. "How about we learn the rest of the layers and their concepts this afternoon and tomorrow morning, and then we decide whether or not to design an intervention?"

Maryann volunteered agreement first. "I'd be comfortable with that."

One by one, they all agreed, but Tom.

"Tom?"

"Can I take the wait-and-see approach?"

"Yes, that is your prerogative."

"All right, then. I will wait to cast my vote until after you've unpacked the content."

"Deal." Glen agreed.

He was 99.9 percent sure Tom would vote yes.

⁓

Glen suggested a new setting. "Who could use a shot of caffeine?"

It was unanimous. So the group headed down to the café.

Laney and Sondra located two tables in a quiet corner and pushed them together, while the rest placed orders. It was a cozy spot for seven.

Glen started by refreshing their memory about the components of the communication model and the importance of checking assumptions.

"As you've seen, effective communication requires a lot of careful thinking. Good communicators think through what content to include in their messages and how the content should be ordered by anticipating the receiver's needs, interests, and concerns."

"Easier said than done," Laney said.

"Yes, indeed, Laney. Mental strategizing is tough. It's what we call framing a message."

"Like framing a house in building construction!" Kate was pleased with herself.

"Nice comparison. The frame is a critical part of the house. And in communication, constructing a thought frame provides context and keeps the receiver's attentions focused on specific aspects for specific reasons. But despite its importance, leaders typically find it the most difficult communication skill to master. Any guesses as to why?"

Sondra was frank. "I've always struggled with framing. I'm not good at establishing what to include or not include or how to sequence the ideas."

Maryann sympathized. "Well, there is a lot to leverage. You have to take people's issues and differences into account."

"Like what?" Tom pushed her further.

"Like who's in the audience and how they learn or how they communicate best, what objections they're going to throw out, what might be affecting their mood. Stuff like that," Sondra said.

"If you have your notepad handy," Glen said, "I have a tool to help you frame messages efficiently."

He waited as they scurried to get set.

"It's P-A-I-B-O-C: purpose, audience, information, benefits, objections, and context. Let's try an exercise. Think of a message you'd like to draft for Jack right now," Glen coaxed. "Something appropriate," he added slyly, which sparked a fresh round of laughter.

He began a litany of questions.

One at a time, Glen read the questions, giving the group plenty of time to think and write.

"What is your purpose in this message?

What do you hope to accomplish?

What do you need to know about your audience?

What vested interest does your audience have?

Who else might see/hear this message?

What key points need to be shared?

What order makes the most sense for this audience?

What information does not need to be included?

What benefits can your audience gain from this message?

How can you emphasize the positive?

How does this message benefit others?

What obstacles might affect how the message is received?

How can you proactively address concerns or obstacles?

What circumstances do you need to keep in mind?

What factors could affect the sending or receiving?"

Glen respected their need to think through these weighty questions. A lot was at stake. He let them work through their ideas alone and hopped up to refill his Diet Coke at the fountain.

As he turned to head back, he watched them collaborate and converse—even with mutual enjoyment. He marveled at the new level of familiarity they reached.

They don't need me, Glen realized. They need one another. My job is to give them some tools to make this office what they want it to be.

He moseyed back and eavesdropped. For the next hour, the group compared ideas and challenged each other's assumptions. They identified key points that outlined their major concerns and sequenced details to support their claims.

But more than anything, their confidence soared. They were no longer alone in this battle.

At a carefully chosen moment, Glen inserted himself into the conversation. "May I share a few thoughts with the group?"

They gladly welcomed his insight.

"It's almost four o'clock now. And we have an hour before we end this first day of training. But already, I've witnessed quite a metamorphosis!" Their relieved faces validated his thinking.

Glen continued. "Before we move into the final portions of communication, I'd like to pose a few thoughts for further reflection. This whole day has been about leadership presence—*your* leadership presence— the way others perceive you based on your behaviors. The choices you make every day collectively reflect you. That's a really big deal: your behaviors largely influence how you're seen. But here's the kicker. We're still only in the third layer. Tomorrow, we'll unpack the last two layers, the innermost layers. They're still connected to the layers from today but in a weightier way."

They were still with him, so he pressed on.

"I remind you of all this so you can take responsibility for yourself—for your own choices and behaviors, to take charge of changing the way others perceive you in order to be a more inspirational, commanding leader."

Glen sensed their hunger for professional excellence. "But it doesn't end with you. I also remind you of these elements so you can begin thinking about how you want Merton Financial–Seattle to be perceived by people inside and outside the organization. So you can begin thinking about what you can do differently or better to enhance the organizational leadership presence."

They reflected for a few seconds before Tom interrupted the concentration.

"Glen, we've all come up with things to say to Jack. We know the message. But how do we express them in a way that will be heard effectively?"

"Ah, mechanics! Yes, a necessary next step in communication. Would you all be open to moving back to the conference room where we began today's training? We'll need some space to move, as we work through the finer points of verbal and nonverbal delivery."

Before Glen finished, they were gathering their things.

In less than a minute, the table sat empty.

∼

Glen stood at the apex of the semicircle, facing the group.

They didn't look as awkward standing together as they had earlier that morning in the lobby entrance. Through the crucible of the afternoon's events, they had become battle ready.

With shoulders back and hips squared, he set about preparing them. "Communication success depends upon two things." Glen held up one finger. "One, framing a solid message," adding a second finger, "and two, delivering the message clearly and eloquently."

Sondra wrestled with self-doubt. Delivering messages had never been her strong suit.

Glen, sensing her nervousness, carried on. "I'm going to share some best practices for verbal and nonverbal delivery with you but not until something is crystal clear."

He grew eerily quiet, far too long for Maryann's taste. She cleared her throat to edge him along. Within a fraction of a second, however, she caught herself and stood erect. Wasn't she going to make every effort to exercise patience, no matter how painful? And effort it required, undeniably so.

Glen's gaze penetrated each of theirs.

"Delivery is not about you. So pay close attention to the feedback you receive from the audience you're trying to reach, and tailor your expression to the audience's needs."

He knew it was a bold risk but chose to take it.

"Sondra, would you be our model for this next portion? I'm looking for a brave soul to demonstrate verbal mechanics."

Yesterday's Sondra would have politely declined the offer. At what point in her career at Merton Financial she had lost her confidence addressing groups, she couldn't say. She'd come to accept the stinging irony. A director of human resources should not be afraid to speak to people.

YOU CAN TAKE RESPONSIBILITY FOR YOURSELF— FOR YOUR OWN CHOICES AND BEHAVIORS, TO TAKE CHARGE OF CHANGING THE WAY OTHERS PERCEIVE YOU IN ORDER TO BE A MORE INSPIRATIONAL, COMMANDING LEADER.

Sondra choked down the dread. "Sure."

Before she could change her mind, she faced the group in the apex, with Glen opposite her in the semicircle.

"Your voice speaks a lot about you, right?" Glen asked.

The semicircle seemed smaller, the group closer. Glen connected with each person.

"Sondra, your voice is naturally appealing."

Her first reaction was to discount the compliment until she saw others nodding.

"Yes, I could listen to her all day," said Laney.

"Mm. Eloquent," Tom agreed.

"Really?" Sondra, incredulous, disagreed. "My voice sounds choppy and hollow and, well, boring to me."

"That's interesting." She could see Miles was being straight with her. "It doesn't sound that way to anyone else."

Perhaps there was some truth to Glen's remark. She gave herself permission to entertain the idea.

Glen held his hands up, ready to conduct the choir. "Let's try a voice experiment, Sondra. I'd like you to describe how you make a peanut butter and jelly sandwich. Lots of details, got it? The goal is for you to speak nonstop."

"You know I'm going to feel ridiculous," Sondra said.

"Probably. But as words come out, I'm going to manipulate the way they sound. Just go with me on this, okay?"

"Only for you, Glen."

Her playfulness encouraged him to press on.

She began the litany of steps.

"First, I walk over to the refrigerator and open the door. Then I locate the loaf of whole wheat bread, not white, and pull it out. With care, I place it on the counter beside the refrigerator."

Engrossed in the details of sandwich-making, Sondra found herself responding in perfect tune to Glen's orders.

"Softer sound."

"More volume."

"Speak at a higher pitch."

"Lower your pitch."

"Now, maintain one pitch."

"Faster tempo."

"Slow down."

"Emphasize every other pitch."

"Pause for dramatic effect."

"Enunciate the words."

"Mumble."

"Drop the final sound of each word."

"Mispronounce a word."

Sondra complied with all his requests, and the observers broke into applause after her performance. Then Glen gave her a high-five.

She hadn't felt that good in a long time.

"What did you learn from Sondra's vocal performance?" The seriousness in Glen's voice redirected attention.

Miles thought before he spoke. "I can see how matching your volume, pitch, and tempo to your circumstances can either display confidence and control or not."

"Yes, and to add to that," Kate said, "varying the way you say something—you know, like Sondra did with sound and speed and pausing and stuff—makes what you say way more interesting."

"I agree, but—" Then in a softer tone, Maryann added her point. "The variance should have purpose. You don't want your voice to sound like a runaway roller coaster."

"Intentional rhythm." Tom summarized aloud.

"Exactly!" Glen affirmed.

Glen was taken aback once again by Tom's reserved insight; he suspected a great deal remained unspoken.

～

Glen then positioned them into two lines, facing one another. The stress from earlier had dissolved. He now walked between partners who genuinely wanted to like each other.

"All right, gang. Verbal mechanics is part of delivery. But what speaks more than your voice and content combined? Your body."

He used himself as the model.

"Your eyes, facial expressions, hands, posture, and movement convey what you're feeling about yourself and your message and most especially your audience. Real quick, now, everyone, show what you would call negative body language."

He stepped between the pairs and issued random comments.

"Check out Maryann's crossed arms. Nice. Tom, great pout. I'm scared at how good you are at rolling your eyes, Laney. Sondra, you're showing me you're closed. Not listening. Yes, yes."

He stepped back away from the group.

"Take a look at each other. Think about the vibe you get from these motions. We send messages to one another all the time with our bodies."

They all started talking at once.

"Great energy." He inserted himself into the pandemonium. "Okay. I'm going to practice some vulnerability here, so everyone, have a seat. Get comfortable."

He continued with directions as they grabbed chairs and found some space. "I'm the monkey in the middle."

"Don't be so hard on yourself." Glen inwardly rejoiced to see Sondra this lighthearted.

"Think back upon the day—all the times you've seen me speak or interact with you. As I cue you on certain aspects of nonverbal behavior, throw out thoughts about what I've done well and what I could improve."

Absorbed, they stared in thought.

Where the average guy would have grown ill at ease, Glen radiated confidence. In fact, he seemed to anticipate enjoyment of what could be an awkward analysis.

"Eye contact." It was Miles.

In general, the Merton Financial team thought Glen's eye contact had been excellent all day. His consistently honest, direct gaze fell upon one person at a time.

No one felt creeped out or ignored, Kate reassured.

"That's comforting!" His grin foretold his trust in them. "What about facial expressions? How effective have mine been?"

Again, the majority of the team noted high levels of satisfaction with Glen's ability to coordinate his facial expressions with his intentions. His masterful control of his features—smiles, raised eyebrows, down-turned mouth, drooping eyes—contributed to the effective reception of his message. As Tom put it, Glen's visible expressions were in sync with his messages.

Only one person dissented. It's not that Maryann disagreed with Glen's talent; she simply preferred low-key responsiveness.

Laney reached out. "I see what you mean, Maryann. Over-the-top dramatics leave a bad taste in my mouth too. But I don't think Glen's been extreme. He's just been alert and attentive with expressions. It certainly has made for a fast day, right?"

Maryann agreed.

And all was well once again.

~

Glen segued into gestures and prefaced the group's comments by clarifying different types. Some hand gestures show transition, such as holding up fingers for one, two, and three. Other gestures display emphasis, such as making a fist or laying palms flat to set the foundation, and other gestures describe realities or even show location: drawing a circle or pointing toward the doorway.

Everyone recalled seeing Glen use all of these gestures throughout the day in purposeful and appropriate ways—never overusing or "hand chopping," as Miles called it.

Then Glen, hands on hips, asked about posture, space, and movement. One at a time, they described his posture as alert and open, well-balanced, and strong. While Kate thought he moved too often, Sondra thought he used movement to his advantage, as if the movements became the transitions.

Miles said, "Yeah. I don't remember any nervous pacing or purposeless walking. Of course, you're a no-nonsense kind of guy."

"Thank you for the compliment, Miles, I think," Glen said.

Glen let the buzz settle before introducing the final segment for the day.

"We've covered a lot this afternoon. Communication from a leadership presence standpoint deals with assumptions, framing, verbal mechanics, and nonverbal delivery. But there's one last, critical communication factor in strong presence. Anyone want to take a guess?"

Only Tom ventured a guess. "Listening?"

"Yes, Tom. Why?"

"Well, listening goes beyond hearing words and abstaining from speaking. It's an act of compassion and care."

"What do you mean?" Maryann tried raising her eyebrows slightly, as she had seen Glen do.

"Real listening is a gift of your attention, time, and concern. It's a heart thing." Tom felt all eyes on him. "Almost everybody thinks he or she is a good listener."

"Go figure!" Miles laughed, shaking his head. "And almost no one feels heard."

"Let me piggyback off Tom and Miles," Glen said. "There are different degrees or levels to our listening. I can merely hear the words, as in their surface value. Even children do this, right? As I become a better listener, I learn to listen for meaning underneath what's being said, and the most mature degree of listening—the deepest level—is where I tap into the emotions and assumptions of the speaker."

"Kate, you look like you want to say something."

"It's just…that…I feel like I have a hard enough time remembering everything a person says from beginning to end. I mean, if I don't jump in and respond when my thought comes to me, I spend the rest of the time thinking about what I'm going to say and not listening. Does this happen to anyone else?"

"I have the same problem, Kate," Laney said. "Especially when I listen to someone who goes on and on."

She chuckled. "I struggle enough with the first level—that basic level of listening you were talking about Glen. Any advice for getting better?"

"For sure, this deepest level requires a highly mature listening ability—the kind where you can hold on to thoughts for the sake of comprehension while simultaneously considering an appropriate response *and* analyzing the unspoken needs, thoughts, and desires of the other person."

"Kind of like mental gymnastics?" Miles suggested.

"Miles, we can always count on you to bring it down to our level." Tom threw him a fist-bump.

"Nice analogy. Gymnastics that take time to develop," Glen said.

Laney said, "I don't have time to wait that long."

"Step by step, Laney. Step by step."

⌢

Glen waited for the chatter to subside.

The weight of the day was now behind him.

"We're down to our last ten minutes. But I'm giving you a listening exercise to practice tonight—a sort of first step in improving listening because, remember, skills can be developed. So, tonight, I want you to have a conversation with someone—anyone, but while you're listening, pay attention to the thoughts going on in your head."

He ignored their goofy remarks and used his voice to keep them focused. "Being mindful of your thoughts and being willing to analyze the what, why, and how of them will give you fascinating insights into how to become a better listener. Okay? Talk, listen, and think. Then be ready to report back tomorrow morning with what you learned. Any questions?"

"Yeah, what are we doing tomorrow?" Maryann called a spade a spade.

"Tomorrow. We'll be digging into the last two layers of leadership presence, the inner layers. We're going deep into the pool, Maryann."

"Will Jack be joining us?" she asked.

Everyone tabled their thoughts for Glen's answer.

Glen answered truthfully. "I don't know. We have plenty to discuss, and I've asked him to attend." He cut short before he said too much.

He directed their attention to preparations.

"I know you began this training today with no expectations and no point of reference. In fact, you were forced to attend." Maryann grinned at his tease.

"Take a few minutes now and write down what has been the most beneficial idea you've gained about your presence as a leader—something you're willing to share with the group. When you're ready, feel free to speak up."

Glen busied himself by tidying up his workspace at the end of the conference table, patiently supporting their need for reflective space.

After close to a minute, Kate piped up first. "My biggest takeaway has been the fact that I *am* a leader, even if I sit at a desk in the front lobby all day. People will see me and watch me. And they will form opinions of our office because of what I present." Her voice cracked. "That's a big job."

Laney could empathize. "Yeah, it's a huge job, Kate. My takeaway is similar. I guess today helped me see that my presence isn't all about me. It's about my ability to connect with other people, and that means my behaviors have to consider other people's needs."

"Thank you, Kate and Laney." Glen smiled. "Others?"

"Mine's different from theirs," Miles said. "A little humiliating, I suppose. I've learned I better step it up a notch. I've gotten kinda lazy, if you know what I mean. As much as I hate to admit it, the details matter in dress and etiquette and stuff."

"I can identify with you, Miles. I, too, have had plenty of aha moments today." Sondra had no problem confessing. "Today, I've been able to see how small things I've left undone, like in my communication with others, have sparked bigger issues. I'm somewhat overwhelmed about what I should improve, but I'm hopeful Glen will get me on the right track."

"Thanks for the honesty, Miles and Sondra. Tom? What are you taking away from today?"

Tom stared at his paper as he answered. "I feel fairly comfortable with what we learned today, but new questions have sprung up in my mind. I want to know how I can be taken seriously as a leader." He shrugged slightly. "A good suit will only go so far. I should know. I've been on the job hunt lately."

Glen let the group chew on Tom's bitter remark. He nodded slowly and then turned to Maryann. "And your takeaway, Maryann?"

She surprised them all. "I need to care more about how I come across to other people." She took their silence as confirmation and rested in the strength it gave.

"Thank you, all, for a great first day."

Glen's voice broke into the quiet and recharged their spirits. "Tomorrow, let's meet back here in the conference room at eight o'clock sharp. Come prepared to share how your listening experiment went. And don't be late. That would be bad manners!"

The noise and bustle dwindled as they each left, drained from a full day.

Glen slumped in a chair and rubbed his temples. He better bring his A-game tomorrow. No holds barred.

He reached for his phone and dialed Jack's number.

Part III: Magnitude

9

~

GUTS BEFORE GLORY

Tom arrived at the conference room first. He'd been up for hours.

Most mornings, his body stirred before his alarm. He'd fallen into the annoying habit over the past year. Stress-induced, most likely. This morning, he crawled out of bed at three o'clock, speculating what the day would bring.

He chose a seat near the front of the conference table and sat, pensive. He sipped the scalding black coffee and tried to exhale out the familiar anxiousness he'd come to anticipate with daybreak.

Glen slipped in, careful not to disturb Tom's calm. But Tom heard and welcomed him. No sense in imposing his restlessness on another.

They made small talk until others began filtering in.

Glen opened his mouth to share news about Jack's expected arrival when his attention derailed. Miles entered sporting a three-piece navy suit—clean, tailored, and sharp. He'd combed and styled his curls, and his face was clean shaven.

"What?" He questioned their staring faces, grinning. "I listened yesterday, okay?"

Everyone, in fact, looked better. Maryann's silk scarf softened her face, and Laney had chosen pumps instead of ballerina flats. Even Kate was transformed. Her cashmere sweater set and pearls spoke: she was pleased to represent Merton Financial–Seattle on the front lines.

Glen felt like a pleased father.

"We have another promising day ahead of us, folks. Refresh your coffee at the table in the back, or grab a bottle of water. Then let's begin where we left off last night." He waited until they'd situated themselves before unveiling the plan.

"First, I'd like you to report what you learned from your listening experiment last night. I think we'll all gain a lot by hearing what worked and didn't work. And after that discussion, we'll move into the fourth layer of presence: gravitas. It will take the lion's share of the morning, leaving the last layer, character, for the afternoon."

His voice dropped. "Jack is planning to be with us during these last two sessions. I actually expected him to be here by now."

Their silence muffled the larger concerns.

Miles spoke first. "At least we're not alone, right? You know. Safety in numbers." The tension broke as the key players of Merton Financial–Seattle looked at one another with relief.

Crusaders hung together.

~

Glen wrote "listening insights" on the board and initiated the debriefing.

Maryann started off with a bang. "I didn't like what I saw in myself. It was ugly, frankly." Glen's kind expression encouraged her to go on.

"All I could think about was how much I wanted other people to stop talking. Once I realized what I was thinking, I felt terrible. I don't even know what I needed to do so badly or why it seemed like such a big deal to keep listening."

"I actually kind of felt the same way. Sort of." Kate offered her shy thoughts next. "I think I just wanted to have my own turn to talk."

"Can you tell us what happened?" Laney asked.

"Sure, I guess. I mean," Kate stumbled. "Well, last night, my boyfriend was telling me about his stressful day, going on and on about different people in his office who are driving him crazy, and all I could think about was how he was doing the very same complaining they were. I found myself getting frustrated, waiting for him to stop talking so that I could tell him my real thoughts."

"Yeah, I do that too." Laney smiled. "Mostly, though, I was super distracted, like with my son. He'll say something, and it will remind me of something else. And before I know it, my mind is a million miles away. Then I have to force myself back and try to figure out what I'd missed." A sad laugh escaped from Laney. "It's pretty pathetic that I've gotten so good at pretending."

Sondra clapped. "I know exactly what you mean. I even tell myself up front to focus!"

Glen steered the small-group conversation to the larger group. "Tom, what insights did you gather from your listening experiment?"

Leaning forward in his chair, and resting his elbows on his knees, Tom spun a pencil in his fingers, around and around. "I'm fairly confident in my ability to listen well. I can weigh a lot of pieces of information in my mind at one time, and I make a point to hear and understand other people."

> GRAVITAS—IT'S THE WEIGHTINESS OR SERIOUSNESS OF YOUR LEADERSHIP. IT'S WHAT MAKES OTHERS RESPECT YOU AND TRUST YOU AND TAKE YOU SERIOUSLY.

He turned to look at each person in the group. "Now, I'm not saying it's easy because it's not. It takes a lot of energy. But where I struggle," he continued, shifting back in his seat, "is being taken seriously. I'm not sure other people notice this ability. Listening well isn't enough." He flung the pencil on the table in front of him.

Glen capitalized on his point. "All of you, I appreciate your transparency."

He bounded out of his seat.

"This is a perfect time to introduce the next layer of gravitas. When you think gravitas, I want you to think gravity, heavy, you know? So we're in the zero-entry swimming pool, right, and we're moving deeper. Think about how that feels. Your toes strain to touch the bottom, and the water's pressing upon you. You lift your chin just to breathe. It's dense and heavy. That's gravitas in presence. It's the weightiness or seriousness of your leadership. It's what makes others respect you and trust you and—"

"—and take you seriously," finished Tom.

"Yes, and take you seriously, yes. Building this distinctive inner layer impacts how others perceive your strength and dependability. But despite its importance to leadership presence, gravitas is easier to identify than define, given the magnitude of each component."

"So what do you suggest we do to boost our gravitas?" Miles emphasized the word *gravitas* with air quotes.

Glen said, "Start with the hardest thing to build and the easiest thing to lose. Your reputation." On the whiteboard, he scratched out, HOW ARE YOU KNOWN? Then he drew a line underneath and numbered one, two, and three.

1. How do I think others see me?

2. How do I want them to see me?

3. What hinders or helps the way they see me?

He spun around. "I'd like you to answer these questions individually. Use your notepad to capture your thoughts, and use these questions to probe your mind and heart. You may or may not like what you find. And that's okay. This exercise is about getting to know yourself intimately, carefully—to gather data about *you* to inform the choices you make."

He stood, shoulders back, chin tilted upward. "Remember, reputation influences gravitas, and gravitas influences presence. And your presence—the way others perceive your behaviors—is largely under your control."

Sondra pressed. "Wait. Before we begin, could you clarify something for me? I'm trying to wrap my mind around gravitas. Okay. It's basically your reputation. Is that all?"

"Yes, that's part of it. Another part of gravitas is your ability to be both confidently assertive and supportively collaborative—a happy marriage between the two."

Glen smiled. "And there's more. Gravitas is also demonstrated in your composure—you know, how calm you can be in the midst of stress or conflict—and your competence. If you don't have the capabilities to lead or get results, the trust other people have in your leadership dwindles."

"Quite a bundle." Tom's mind reeled.

"So back to this HOW ARE YOU KNOWN question… How much time do we get? A day?" Miles asked.

"I wish we had that much time, Miles. It takes time to open yourself up to be that vulnerable. How much time would you like, everyone?"

Kate reasoned aloud. "Thirty minutes should be enough time to generate good thoughts. May we go somewhere private?"

"Yes, definitely. Take your things. Find a quiet place where you can reflect with honesty—"

Before he finished, the door flew open. A shadow fell across the room.

Sondra caught the glint in Glen's eye.

"Glad you could finally join us, Jack."

～

Jack didn't bother to move as the group filed past him. But he also didn't make a point to look them in the eye.

"You're late," Glen said, rummaging through his briefcase.

"I arrived, didn't I?" Jack shot back.

"Not according to our agreement. Have a seat, Jack." Impatience slipped into Glen's voice.

Jack sauntered over to a back seat by the window and flopped down. "So what do you want me to do?"

Glen stared at him, lost in thought until Jack squirmed uncomfortably under the hot light of truth. "What already?"

Glen reached for an unused notepad sitting by his briefcase. He wrote out some ideas, closed the pad, and walked it back to Jack.

"I want you to think about these questions and answer them as honestly as you can." He added with force: "Write out your answers."

A skeptical Jack snatched the pad and opened to the front page. He read both questions aloud. "How seriously does your team take you as a leader? Would they follow you into the fire?"

He exploded. "What kinds of questions are these?"

"You figure it out. You're a smart guy."

Glen turned back to his briefcase and gathered his things.

"I'll be back in thirty minutes. And I'll look forward to hearing your thoughts."

"Glen!" Jack hollered.

The door clanged shut.

Jack faced his thoughts. Alone.

～

Sondra came back first.

She could have used more time to reach the depths of reflection the question deserved, now that she finally faced its invitation. In all honesty, she'd been afraid to know the answer; she would rather live in the pretense that all was okay. By habit, Sondra bypassed uneasy topics.

She figured others had finished and rushed back to the conference room to keep them from waiting for her. So entering, to see Jack, startled her.

She stole her seat, not wishing to wake the sleeping giant. Her back faced Jack. She could feel his eyes burning into her, yet she remained rigid in her seat. She didn't have the emotional stamina to entertain a potentially volatile conversation.

One by one, others returned. She concentrated on deep breaths to slow her heartbeat. Inhale. Exhale. One, two, three, four. It had already been a heavy morning.

No one talked much. The busyness of shuffling papers, yawning, and glancing at the clock gave the appearance of nonchalance. But nothing could be further from reality due to Jack's icy presence.

Glen rushed in, breaking through the thickness. He apologized for keeping them waiting, his fresh enthusiasm galvanizing them.

"Welcome back! I hope you had some valuable think time."

He plunged right into the thick of things. "So as you've been thinking, I've been thinking."

He placed his tablet down and dragged a chair into the center of the U-shaped table.

"You've been reflecting on your reputation—how you're known, the weightiness of your leadership, the respect others have for you, that kind of thing. Gravitas is all of this hefty stuff, you know, and it impacts the trust others place in you."

He could tell they were with him. Even Jack kept his eyes on Glen.

"But here's the rub. Here's where the layers begin to bleed together."

He turned back to the board and drew the presence model once again. "See how this fourth layer, gravitas, wraps itself around character, the fifth layer? They are individual, unique layers, yes, but gravitas is firmly supported by character. If character—which is the core of the model, you'll notice—is weak or shallow, gravitas loses robustness. It becomes flabby or unsteady."

Maryann, absorbed in thought, spoke loud enough for Glen to hear. "Character is the linchpin."

"That's a creative way of looking at it, Maryann."

Glen moved back to his chair and sat forward with his elbows resting on his knees. He was the coach addressing his players.

"A person can have impressive style, impeccable etiquette, effective communication, and even a serious personal brand, but if his character is flawed, his leadership presence falls short of inspiring trust that others place in him. His credibility as a leader is at stake."

"What about the other way around?" Tom threw out the question foremost on his mind. "Say a person's character is solid, but he lacks competence or composure. Can his character compensate?"

"Yes and no. How's that for clear as mud?" Glen responded with a grin. "Yes, character bears the greatest weight of all the layers. But it's not an island. All the other layers of the model work together to portray the richness of the core."

"Remember the zero-entry swimming pool?" Maryann proudly threw out.

"Yes, yes, I remember. It's just that, well, where does a person start? I mean, all of this is overwhelming," Tom said. He looked down for a few seconds before continuing. "I've always tried to maintain strong character. I believe in its importance, and so if other things went by the wayside, at least I could know that my core was strong. Was I wrong in my thinking?"

Glen couldn't ignore the magnitude of Tom's transparency.

"Tom, I commend your thinking for a number of reasons."

He softened his voice and leaned in. "On one hand, you uphold and exercise what matters most: character. It's a lot simpler to adjust behavior regarding style or etiquette than to implement new habits involving our value system."

Relief washed over Tom's face.

"On the other hand, you recognize that you possess opportunities for growth. We all do."

He spread his hands out to the group and then patted his palm on his chest. "This guy included. That's the point of our two-day training. My job has been to introduce you to the layers of leadership presence so you can take inventory on how you're doing and determine a personal development plan to boost the strength and authenticity of your leadership."

"Now hold your horses, Glen." Jack's voice sliced through the calm that had been infiltrating the room. "That's not what we talked about." Jack reared up out of his seat.

Glen raised a firm hand. "Jack. Let me finish sharing some insights with the group, and then you and I can talk over lunch." He waited for a response. "Fifteen minutes, tops."

Jack glared. "Fifteen minutes. I'll be in the hall waiting." He turned on his heels and slammed the door behind him.

"Where was I?" Glen caught his breath and stared at the floor.

"I think you were going to cue us up for a character discussion with Jack," Sondra hinted.

Glen took the bait. "Right," nodding. "That's exactly what I was going to do."

He didn't waste a minute.

10

~

BATTLE PLANS

Kate decided now was a good time to bail.

"Look, I get that a lot of people are unhappy with what's been going on in this office. And I get that Jack's a little twisted about what's important. But I am not seeing how my behavior changes are going to make a dent in the culture here. I mean, I spent a hundred bucks on this sweater last night, but so far, things are worse today than they were yesterday. And now you're throwing out the idea of a discussion with Jack about character, and I'm not even sure I know what character means or whether or not I want to be a part of the conversation."

She shook her head in apology and paused. "Sorry. I know this is all random and negative. But I'm new here, and I need this job. I don't want to be a part of something that's going to jeopardize my future."

Laney stepped in. "Kate, I share your concerns. I'm also feeling uneasy about where this is headed. Glen, maybe you could give us some perspective."

"Of course. There's a missing piece to be addressed, Kate, in order for next steps to become clear. And that is the character piece," Glen said.

"That would be great, Glen," Miles said. "Character seems hazy and ginormous."

A VIRTUE IS A HABITUAL DISPOSITION TO DO GOOD.

"Right. Let's start back at the beginning. Presence, you recall, is basically behavioral expression. Your behaviors over time and across situations and contexts not only influence how others perceive your leadership capabilities, but characterize you; they mark you. So your character contains all the qualities that make up you—traits, values, and virtues. And these qualities are manifested through what you say and do."

"A trait? Like a personality trait?" Laney pursued her question. "Like a sense of humor?

"Sure," Glen said. "And values represent what you hold dear or worthy. For example, if a person values family and work ethic, he places high importance upon them."

"And then what is a virtue? How is it different from a value?" Laney asked.

"Right. So a virtue is a habitual disposition to do good. If I make a regular practice of telling the truth, I've developed the virtue of honesty."

Maryann's brow furrowed. "There's a lot involved in character."

Glen sympathized. "Yes, so to make things simple, we can focus on two major aspects of character particularly associated with leadership presence that inspire others' trust and confidence in you: integrity and intent."

He reached over to the table for his notepad and drew a large circle and flashed it before the group.

"To be a person of integrity is to be a person of wholeness—with no division, incongruence, or partiality. A completeness exists with all parts integrated, and the soundness of the person's character is stronger because of this unity," he said.

Sondra lit up. "I like to think of integrity as being who you say you are and doing what you'll say you'll do."

"Nice! Your thoughts, words, and actions match what you value and believe to be morally good and right. You can imagine, then, how important it is for leaders to know their values—and the values of their organizations. Otherwise, they have no compass to guide them."

Miles chuckled. "My dad used to say that you better stand for something, or you'll fall for anything."

"Sounds like a country-western song," Laney teased.

Glen ignored the laughter and sketched on the notepad. The banter ceased as they watched him, engrossed. He flipped over the pad to show a giant equal sign with a V on one side and an A on the other.

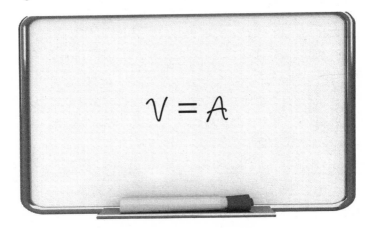

"Leaders with high character demonstrate congruence between what they value—that's the *V*—and what they do. I've drawn it here as an *A*. Their values and actions sync up. Okay. We've got that: congruence occurs internally, meaning, their personal behaviors match up with their personal value set. Yet congruence also happens externally, and that's when their behaviors align with the ethical values expected by their organization."

Glen opened his mouth to continue his explanation when Sondra burst out. "That's it!"

Everyone stared at her.

"That's the problem! Do you guys see it?"

"Problem?" Maryann asked cautiously.

"Merton Financial–Seattle has no ethical expectations of its employees. We have no compass. No discussions, no clarity, no consistency. We pretty much all act the way we think we're supposed to act—or the way we want to act. But how confusing is that?"

Sondra's comment opened a floodgate.

Everyone began talking over one another until Glen reined them back in.

"You're onto something here, and you deserve time to discuss this issue more deeply. But let's talk about the second aspect of character so you can consider the full picture."

With energy brimming over, they listened as Glen explained how leaders act from motivation—that intention drives everything they do. And he challenged them to consider their own why, how, and what.

"Why are you motivated to act?" Glen asked. "How do you plan to activate your motive? And what behaviors will you use to execute your plan? These are the questions leaders should seriously consider in order to develop relational transparency."

"Relational what?" Miles asked.

Kate answered, "It means you're real with people. And you're real with yourself."

"Well said, Kate."

Glen took a green marker and wrote A-C-C-O-U-N-T-A-B-I-L-I-T-Y on the board. "What does this have to do with character?"

"Everything," Tom responded right away.

"Speak to us more about that, Tom."

"Accountability is self-discipline," he said. "It's holding yourself to your intentions and commitments. I guess we could say it's what holds integrity and intent in working order."

He opened himself up to the group. "I owe everyone here an apology. Too many times, I failed to hold others accountable, but more often than not, I failed to hold myself accountable. It was easier to overlook or ignore what I said I would do or should have done. I realize my time is up here, but I am learning from my mistakes. I hope to be a better leader because of them."

Sometimes preserving silence is the best action. But a soft knock on the door broke the stillness.

Angelina from the front desk cracked the door open and peeked into the room.

Kate gushed, surprised. "Why, Angelina! Is everything okay down front?"

"Yes, all is well." Her sunny disposition filled the room.

"But Mr. Jack Merton asked me to give Mr. O'Brien a message." She cleared her throat before continuing. Kate pointed to Glen who stood.

"Ah, Mr. O'Brien, he would like you to come down to the entrance as soon as possible. He wanted me to be sure to let you know it's been twenty-three minutes."

She then dropped her voice into a whisper. "He's a little upset."

"Thank you for the message, Angelina. Please let him know we're finishing up now. I'll be down soon."

Angelina obliged, brimming with pleasant charm. Glen rallied the group one last time.

"We made it through the overview. You know what you need to know about leadership presence. Now, it's up to you to decide where you want to go with this training."

He checked the clock. "Food should be arriving shortly for lunch, and as you've heard, I've been summoned downstairs."

He appreciated their grins.

"I'm passing the baton to you. Spend this next hour deciding how to take Merton Financial–Seattle in the direction you want it to go. You're the leaders."

Guilt gripped his heart as he gathered his belongings. But their stares didn't diminish the conviction he had that they solve their own problems in light of what they'd learned about leadership and themselves.

"We'll be back in one hour," and he dashed out the door.

A faint "Good luck!" followed him to the elevators.

But before he could push the arrow, the doors opened. Jack stood with arms crossed.

~

Jack held back his impatience with clenched teeth.

He waited for Glen to slip alongside him in the elevator, shoulder to shoulder, waiting for the golden doors to close before unloading.

He'd spent a fortune flying Glen here for two weeks to fix the drama in the messed-up office. Instead, he'd watched Glen brainwashing folks with talk about dress and communication. So far, no problems had been solved. No one had been reprimanded or written up. Nothing had changed. In fact, everything was worse. He'd wasted his time and money.

Jack fumed as Glen listened in silence.

His ranting continued even after they left the elevator and headed toward Glen's rental car. They stood on opposite sides of the car, Glen at the driver's door waiting for Jack to finish.

Wrung out and self-conscious, Jack stopped spewing and stared across the roof of the car at Glen.

"What?" His sneer covered years of insecurity.

Awkwardness festered a few seconds before Glen returned a pressing scrutiny with cold eyes.

"Jack Merton, have you ever given any thought to the fact that you might be a huge part of the problem?"

He clicked the key fob and slipped into the driver's seat, leaving Jack dumbfounded.

Glen started the car and let it idle as he rolled down the passenger window. "Get in, Jack. It's your turn to listen."

A now-pensive Jack Merton opened the door and slumped in.

The tables had turned.

Part IV: Mercy

11

~

IN THE DEEP END
OF THE POOL

Dealing with difficult people was nothing new for Glen.

Invincible calm and practical reasoning, he had learned, did wonders. Too much was at stake now with Jack to not ace this deliberate encounter.

He put the car in gear and checked his rearview mirror before backing out of the parking stall. Out of the corner of his eye, he could see Jack, staring straight ahead, absently picking at the cuticle of his left thumb. A telltale sign of nerves.

And so Glen began his address, using every ounce of presence he could muster.

He relayed his original concerns about Jack's request for Glen to fix Merton Financial–Seattle people.

He unveiled reasons for his hesitancy, rooted in Jack's notorious disregard for others he perceived as obstructing his path.

He shared his alarm regarding the isolation and disjointedness of the Seattle members he'd discovered upon his arrival and the excitement that dawned in seeing the potential in their dormant talents.

He emphasized how receptive they'd become with his encouragement and positive support and the hunger he noticed in them to be better than they were.

But mostly, he bore down on Jack.

Did Jack realize how others saw him?

Did he realize why they saw what they saw?

Did he realize the role he played in their perceptions?

Did he realize that only he could change their view?

Real, honest questions.

Down to the deep end of the swimming pool.

~

Miles moved the last chair into place and asked, "How does it look?"

Laney stepped back to survey the arrangement. Two angled lines of chairs formed a V with a single chair positioned in the middle of the wide opening. The U-shaped tables butted neatly against the back wall, while underneath lay seven piles of personal belongings. They'd cleared away the beverage table and wiped off the whiteboards so that only bare tabletops and chairs remained. The room felt sterile and cold.

She was blunt. "It looks like he's going to get initiated."

"Oh, he's going to get initiated all right," said Maryann, "into the Welcome to Reality club."

The three of them cracked up until Sondra shushed them.

"Come on now! Remember why we're doing this. We want Jack to take responsibility for what he can control. Same with us. We've all decided to step it up ourselves, right? We're all in this together."

They knew she was right. Over the lunch hour, they'd come to an agreement to change and be changed—to become who they needed to be so Merton Financial–Seattle could be what they wanted it to be. Yet despite the miraculous metamorphosis that had occurred in twenty-four hours, they were still so entrenched in the current matters to grasp its profundity.

Tom motioned for everyone to be seated. "We better get moving. It's nearly one. They'll be here any minute."

They hustled to their strategic places.

The far left corner of the V was reserved for Glen; he'd be overseeing the intervention. Miles, the facilitator, sat to the right of Glen's chair, and then Kate was immediately to the right of Miles. Maryann placed herself at the point of the V, appropriate to her role as fulcrum. Laney was seated to the right of Maryann, on the righthand side with Tom to her right. At the uppermost point of the right side sat Sondra; she'd be the final speaker. Every position had a purpose.

Kate finished seating herself when Glen whisked open the door. The afternoon sun shone through the windows, magnifying the intensity of the scene, and he batted his eyes to adjust.

He searched out Miles. "Are you ready for us?"

Miles nodded and signaled Glen's entrance.

Just behind Glen's broad shoulders appeared a different Jack in the doorway.

His tie hung loose about his neck, and he held his jacket in his fist. His crisp shirt cuffs were pushed up into makeshift rolls at his elbows. And flecks of gray at his temples accentuated his ashen face.

His slowed pace matched his gaze—strained, weary, open. With eyes half-raised, he found the seat Miles offered him and turned to see everyone before sitting down.

Something had softened in him. Or broken.

They couldn't help but stare.

No one knew what to say. They could only wonder at the nature of his lunch conversation with Glen.

The idea of confronting Jack in this pitiful state now seemed almost cruel and unnecessary.

Yet it was necessary.

Glen, seated in the far left corner of the V, motioned with his head for Miles to begin.

It was now or never.

∼

Miles clarified the procedures.

Each person would have ten minutes to share concerns about the organization and personal plans for improvement. After the group finished its individual sharing, Jack could take some time to reflect and respond.

But no one would leave until consensus was reached regarding the direction of improvement for Merton Financial–Seattle.

No one had any questions or protests. Not even Jack.

∼

One by one, the Merton Financial employees laid bare their personal frustrations with the state of affairs in Seattle. They spoke of what was lacking in their development and their plans to sharpen their presence as leaders in an organization they wished to grow. But more than anything, each speaker sent a bullet straight to Jack's heart: he had not been the leader he could be.

And so they went around the *V*, speaking what had been dormant for far too long.

Miles expressed sorrow for his casualness as the VP of marketing. He had taken its importance for granted and had shirked many responsibilities that, if redressed now, could really put the office back into the Seattle market playing field. They had a great thing going, if only he step it up a notch and be the robust image they wanted to present.

"But, Jack," said Miles, almost as a plea, "couldn't you recognize the value I *do* bring to the organization and help me maximize it instead of belittling me with sarcasm?" Miles strained to catch Jack's attention. Their eyes met for a brief second before Miles pushed out of his seat to get a bottle of water.

The rest of the monologues followed suit.

Kate described her pride at working for a reputable company like Merton Financial. She loved greeting people and assisting them, connecting them with others. But this training had opened her eyes to levels of development that hadn't been happening—development she eagerly wanted in order to be her best for the organization. She wanted to cultivate leadership presence.

"Jack, don't you see that I *matter* to this company? I'm the first person people meet when they enter. Investing in my development is more critical than ever for us to be the organization we believe Merton Financial–Seattle is. Aren't I worth it?" Jack glanced up to catch Kate's plea. He blinked a few times and then looked away.

Maryann spoke next.

She thanked the group members for helping her see the ripple effect of her behaviors. She wasn't an island, though she'd acted like one. For sure, she still had a lot to learn about people skills, but at least she was beginning to recognize the importance of kindness and professionalism.

With bold abandon, she faced her boss of over twenty years, hands on hips. "Jack, why can't you lead by example? How come you've allowed me to get away with rudeness? Come to think of it, I have probably learned many of my habits from you. You know, you're not above all this." Jack kept his eyes fixed on the ground; he didn't flinch.

Laney added her thoughts to the mix. Her understanding of financials was crystal clear. In fact, everyone in the group had the competence essential for excellence. But until Glen came, she had never considered herself a leader. She just did her own thing and expected others to do theirs. And so, if she was going to develop her leadership, she might as well become someone worth following, someone consistent and intentional.

"Jack, what can you do as my leader to hold me more accountable for my results and those of the people I supervise? Right now, it doesn't seem like you care a whip about me or what I do. But you sure do expect perfection, and I never seem able to meet your standards."

He cleared his throat and held up a finger, as if preparing to speak. Laney turned away and reached into her purse for a Kleenex.

Tom allowed for a dramatic pause and then sat forward in his seat, speaking from the heart. He had fallen short as a leader. Everyone in the group had been affected by his weaknesses and insecurities in some way. Though his character remained true and authentic during his time at Merton Financial, it appeared weak and unsteady. No one could confidently trust that kind of leader.

"Jack, if we were to do it all again, I'd prefer you coach me and challenge me—help me see I have potential worth developing. I do best with positivity." Jack suppressed a smirk with a shake of his head until he noticed Tom's rueful stare and then stopped.

Sondra scanned the group, the last to speak. She cleared her throat and swallowed hard.

Her experience at Merton Financial–Seattle had been unique compared to the rest of the group. Unlike them, she'd felt cared for and respected, for the most part, and she clearly saw her instrumental role in the organization as director of human resources. Because she'd hired them all, she had confidence in their unique talents and skill sets; she knew what Merton Financial–Seattle was capable of becoming. But somewhere along the way, she'd lost the ability to clarify expectations. She'd underutilized good communication to keep everyone moving in the same direction and to keep values in view. She'd forsaken them as a liaison.

"Jack, you *have* made me feel included in the organizational mission, and I thank you for that. It's just that, well, you're selective about who you invest in and who you don't. You play favorites, which has complicated my interactions with Merton Financial employees and made it challenging to know if and when to trust you. How can I help you become more consistent in your expectations of all people in the organization and the way you hold them accountable?"

Sondra let her final question set before Jack. She let her words and all those before hers wash over him and seep in.

No one spoke. No one moved. They merely strained with hope that he had heard their meaning.

After moments of silence, Jack lifted his weary head to find seven sets of eyes watching him, expectant.

A flood of thoughts washed over him. Memories of his encounters with them—the arguments, sneers, rash thoughts. Swirls of angry thoughts punctuated his mind and then burst into disappointment. This wasn't how things were supposed to be, not what he wanted, what he had envisioned for Merton Financial. Remorse settled in, heavy, eventually cascading into regret and pouring forth as sadness. He sat spent.

Brutal honesty pierces first, then heals.

He'd endured over sixty minutes of well-organized, well-chosen criticism. Only a man of intense stoicism could leave such a trial unmoved.

But Jack was not that man.

He did the only thing he could do. He put his head in his hands and surrendered.

PART V: PUTTING IT ALL TOGETHER

12

~

MEMO TO JACK

TO: Jack Merton

FROM: Glen O'Brien

SUBJECT: Assessment Report of Seattle
Presence Training

As is customary in a consult, this report synthesizes my assessment of the situation at Merton Financial–Seattle at the time of your phone call three weeks ago, the major factors at play, the key insights gained, and recommendations for continued progress.

Having experienced dysfunctional disillusionment that comes from underdevelopment, as you observed in that branch, the Seattle employees have gained an appreciation for the capacity of inspiration, trust, and satisfaction possible when wholly integrated presence runs at full capacity. It has been a pleasure to assist in their training.

CONTEXTUAL BACKGROUND

From the start, it was my goal to guide them in discovering the authenticity possible in their leadership—what and who they could be. And through their own initiative, they implemented behavioral changes that influenced lasting impressions for them individually and as an organization. I'll expand on that shortly.

Leadership presence is not elusive; it's developmental. It's the totality of your behavioral expression. Targeting specific presence behaviors can leverage your impact and improve how you are perceived because what you do expresses what you value. If you want to be perceived differently, you must think and act differently.

The Leadership Presence Model that I use is a comprehensive visual of five competency areas that enhance a person's leadership presence. The five layers work together collectively to portray the essence of behavioral expression; each distinctive layer is still integral to the whole. Yet to understand the fullness of presence and the interrelatedness of the competency areas, a person can benefit from exploring each separately. You will recall we tackled each of these layers during the training sessions.

LEADERSHIP PRESENCE COMPETENCY AREAS

Let's review each layer separately. The following sections provide an overview of the five major competency areas and points of application for you and your Seattle employees.

Style: Style encompasses major areas such as grooming, dress, environment, and wellness. As the outermost layer of the model, its purpose is to set the first stage of impression—to be the aesthetic introduction of a person. Your physical presence is the first experience others have of you. Jack, you have always demonstrated a first-rate example in this area with your impeccable image, sharp sense of style, and solicitous care of physical details.

As you know, presenting your best appearance means crafting a style that attracts, appeals, and speaks to your quality. Clean, appropriate, and meticulous style tells others you are orderly and conscientious, that you respect details and image. Your outward form sends messages to others about how much you care for and respect yourself, your position, and your organization.

However, the Seattle employees were lacking a shared understanding of your expectations of their attire, and the inconsistency and noncompliance (though unintentional) became a source of irritation and disunity. Sondra, the director of human resources, now has clearer guidelines for keeping everyone abreast of universal expectations of this business professional setting.

Some simple suggestions for maximizing your employees' sense of style include the following:

- Make personal hygiene a priority.
- Pay attention to the details of your appearance.
- Seek to align your style with your organization's culture.
- Dress for the position you want.
- Minimize distractions in your appearance and attire.

- Consider how you appear to others.

- Assess your physical, mental, and spiritual health.

- Recognize that style is a beginning, not an end.

Because style is already a strength for you, Jack, I recommend you build upon the successes already begun in your team and dedicate time and energy to clarifying and upholding expectations built upon shared understanding.

Etiquette: Etiquette represents the second layer of the Leadership Presence Model. It involves thoughtful attention to tactical behaviors that increase others' comfort with you, specifically in the areas of manners, dining, networking, and e-professionalism.

In spending time with your employees, I witnessed firsthand their receptiveness to mastering the expected social conventions. For the most part, lapses in manners and etiquette were a result of lack of training; employees simply didn't know how to behave in specific circumstances or were not aware of how their unconventional (even inappropriate) behavior was being perceived.

Nuanced moves help you smoothly navigate social dynamics and reinforce others' confidence in your presence. So whether you are meeting someone for the first time, encountering a person in the hall, greeting guests at a meal, initiating a conversation between two clients, or posting a blog on the company website, you want to master social protocol that demonstrates your savviness. Etiquette showcases your social grace and willingness to know and understand people.

As the leader of the organization, Jack, you are responsible for setting the supreme example of courtesy, etiquette, and professionalism in any occasion. Your ability to smoothly interact with people should be based upon a profound realization of the dignity others inherently possess and your responsibility in upholding this dignity. Your employees' level of social sophistication is largely determined by what they see you exhibit. Thus, the onus is on you.

Here are my recommendations for developing the areas of competency in etiquette:

- Smile at everyone.
- Demonstrate your appreciation with thanksgiving.
- Call people by name.
- Develop a firm, confident handshake.
- Be courteous of others' time and contributions.
- Practice proper dining etiquette before, during, and after a meal.
- Connect talented, skilled people with one another.
- Ask people to help you get better.
- Think before you post or hit "send."

Remember that people benefit from repetition and gentle reminders as they learn to navigate social situations. Allow them multiple opportunities to practice. Catch them doing well and live the example you expect to see others display.

Communication: Strong communicators have learned to orchestrate the subtleties of message sending and receiving. They recognize the myriad of factors that can impact the way a message is constructed, sent, and received, and they take proactive measures to ensure smooth transmission to advance understanding.

Because of inconsistent messages due to unchecked assumptions and biases, ineffective delivery skills, and poor listening, communication among the employees and between you and the employees has resulted in misunderstanding, disengagement, and disrespect.

For example, crafting an effective message is more than composing words. It starts with thinking—more precisely, acknowledging and checking the assumptions that shape your perspective. Inspirational leaders make a point to identify and clarify assumptions to alleviate confusing or unreasonable expectations in their interactions with others. All employees now more clearly see the need to recognize and evaluate their assumptions, as well as more attentively recognizing receivers' needs.

With careful attention to the audience's style, needs, and vested interests, the communicator can then frame the message and deliver it with a polished voice and open, expressive body language. These mechanical and technical touches accentuate the quality of the message and encourage engagement with the receiver(s).

Tying all communication activity together is attentive listening accompanied by feedback. This reciprocal give-and-take increases the accuracy of message transmission and strengthens the relationship between sender and receiver. While we did work on elements of effective verbal and nonverbal delivery, I highly recommend ongoing training as a critical component of professional development of all members of your team. A person cannot spend too much time learning how to communicate better.

Based on what I noticed with the Seattle employees, here are some specific suggestions to maximize communication efficacy:

- Consider the expectations you hold of other people.
- Reflect upon the assumptions behind these expectations.
- Ask clarifying questions to ensure accuracy.
- Be clear about your purpose and desired outcome for communicating.
- Think about the audience's needs, interests, and concerns when constructing a message.
- Polish your vocal mechanics (such as pitch, volume, tone, tempo, enunciation, and emphasis).
- Read more to improve your vocabulary.
- Assess your poise and physical stature.
- Ask others to evaluate your facial expressions, gestures, and eye contact.
- Look people in the eye when they speak to you.
- Listen to understand what's below the surface of what's being said.

The more expert you can become at reading people and learning to understand what they're saying and where they're coming from, the more they will feel heard, understood, and valued. Then effective communication will become a shared goal.

Gravitas: Gravitas comes from the Latin root *gravis*, meaning heavy, weighty, serious, or important. Positioned toward the center of the Leadership Presence Model, it supports and sharpens the upper layers. Even though all competency areas of the model work together, this deeper area holds a special weight of its own. Without gravitas, others will not take you seriously.

Deep seriousness in your leadership—or lack of it—actually manifests itself through your visible exterior—your style, etiquette, and communication. As a leader, you will either instill confidence in others' trust of you or not. Gravitas is heavily tied to the ability of other people to respect and trust that you (1) know what needs to be done and how to do it (competence); (2) can bring clarity and calm to situations of chaos or conflict (composure); and (3) manage your reputation (how you are known). And so, displaying this wholesomeness in your leadership presence inspires trust in what you can and will do and whom you portray yourself to be. The deep substance of gravitas is based upon unwavering, purposeful commitment to leading oneself and others; it gets to the heart of what you do.

Building this distinctive inner layer impacts how others perceive your strength and dependability. To be taken seriously as a leader, you must become someone with a legacy that confirms your capabilities, courage, and fidelity. Your personal brand—the way you have come to be known—rests upon a respectable foundation as you grow in composure and competence.

Jack, certain members of your team—Tom, for instance—lacked gravitas and lost your respect. As leader of the organization, take the responsibility upon yourself to help your employees attain the development necessary to grow in competence and composure to improve the seriousness others will attach to their leadership. A respectful reputation as a leader is painstaking and time-consuming to build but quickly lost. Your employees will be more inclined to magnify their gravitas when they recognize the value you place on their deep, professional substance.

Here are some specific suggestions for developing gravitas:

- Remember that other people watch you.
- Put forth particular care in managing your personal brand.
- Strive to marry your assertiveness with collaboration.
- Pay attention to how you treat all people.
- Develop your emotional intelligence competencies.
- Practice regular inward reflection.
- Take stock of your talents, skills, and abilities.
- Seek ongoing development of your skills, talents, and abilities.
- Be a goal setter and execute upon the goals you set.
- Assess your results.
- Work toward ongoing progress in your capabilities.
- Maintain a developmental mindset.
- Take your job, position, and leadership seriously.

Be strong and proactive about developing potential in people who work with you.

Character: Character, the innermost layer of the model, is the most consequential to how others perceive your leadership presence. It consists of your traits, values, and virtues, all manifested through what you say and do. In fact, your behaviors over time and across situations and contexts not only influence how others perceive your leadership capabilities but characterize you; they mark you. Jack, it was this layer that presented the most concerns—not so much from your Seattle employees but from you.

Two aspects of credible character directly related to leadership presence are integrity and intent. Integrity implies wholeness and congruence; it's a completeness that integrates all parts of you. Leaders with strong presence aspire to internal and external congruence so that all their thoughts, words, and actions align with their personal values, as well as those of their organization. They avoid compartmentalizing their public and private lives and, instead, hold firm and true to their convictions.

Your team members shared concerns they had regarding your willingness to practice congruence in thought, word, and behavior with them and with yourself. Because they laid out their personal concerns in our intervention session, I will not recount them here. But do realize how widespread and deep-seated character flaws can be in a leader's interactions with others.

Keep in mind that leaders of high character also seek purity and transparency in their intentions. They pay attention to why they are motivated to act, how they plan to activate their motive, and what behaviors they'll use to execute the plan. Their personhood is genuine, and their candor comes across in their willingness to be vulnerable with others—to let others see as they see. They then hold themselves accountable to their responsibilities, commitments, and promises. In other words, they do what they say they will do.

Jack, I suggest you build in a routine for regular, intense reflection, where you examine your motives in light of your thoughts, words, and behaviors. Do your behaviors present who you truly are, who you want to be?

Granted, character is not solely your responsibility; all members of your team implicate their presence by the deepest competency area of the model: character. Nonetheless, you set the expectations for the level of integrity and intention tolerated and even encouraged in your organization.

Strong character takes a lifetime to develop, but here are some concrete ways to make improvements in an area of significant importance:

- Appreciate that each person has a mixed bag of character strengths that distinguish him or her from others.

- Remember that all of your behaviors are either elevating or deescalating the quality of your character.

- Know your values, principles, and convictions.

- Align what you say with what you do.

- Be consistent in acting upon your values and principles rather than compromising.

- Remain self-aware of the intentions behind your actions.

- Practice relational transparency—authentic honesty in your relationships.

- Hold yourself accountable to what you said you'd do.

This layer represents the toughest, deepest competency areas. But more than any of the other layers, it's character that illuminates the others. A leader can dress well, navigate social situations gracefully, even say all the right things in all the right ways, but if the leader's character is underdeveloped or inconsistent or shady, his or her entire presence is affected. Trust, security, and respect are then snuffed out by uncertainty, distrust, and disunity.

SUMMARY

Leadership presence is the outcome of all you think, say, and do and the means by which others will perceive you. The aura you present, however, is not a matter of chance; rather, it is chiefly under your control.

Leadership presence done well looks easy. Though in reality, commanding attention, inspiring rapport, and gracefully executing—leadership presence in action—come from the fusion of five competency areas displayed in the Leadership Presence Model. Setting the gold standard of leadership requires ongoing, purposeful development—efforts leading to legacy.

I direct these final words to you personally, Jack. You have a strong team with high potential. Their openness and receptivity during our training sessions testify to their aptitude for reaching increased levels of success. If you commit to the leadership presence development of yourself and your employees, you can expect a restoration of impressiveness that illustrates the Merton ideal.

13

~

THE REST OF THE STORY

As best practice, Glen followed up with past clients.

Depending on the situation's severity, he'd check in with clients one week, one month, three months, six months, and even one year to evaluate traction. Had they been able to maintain progress?

In the Merton Financial–Seattle case, he touched base at all checkpoints. The tenuous state of affairs prior to his arrival had taken a toll on everyone involved; he'd witnessed their wounds. And knowing what he did about leadership presence, it was too expansive and too deep an issue to work itself out unsupervised.

Yet at each of the evaluative checkpoints, what Glen discovered reassured him that transformation had taken root.

Trust had been restored in Seattle.

~

After the intervention, change came about slowly.

Jack took some time off to reevaluate his priorities

but not before installing Tom as interim president in his absence.

Jack came back renewed and reinvigorated, more humble and more refined—ready to take Merton Financial–Seattle in an upward direction. His ad hoc leadership team was happy to oblige.

Miles crafted a new marketing campaign to position the Seattle office as "present and ready for you."

Kate was promoted to supervise and train all service staff, coaching them to be the face of the Seattle branch—to ensure excellence with every encounter.

Laney assumed responsibility as resident mentor. She worked alongside all incoming employees to support their transition into the presence culture and to instill in them ownership for their own leadership skill development.

Maryann transplanted herself back to the headquarters in Chicago. She called herself the at-large member of the leadership team and established a renewal initiative to integrate leadership presence development in all Merton Financial satellite locations.

With Jack's permission, she asked Tom to join her in these efforts as director of development and training once his interim presidency term was up.

He declined. Though grateful for the opportunity to heal wounds, Tom utilized the leadership presence training as a platform to launch his career in a new direction once his interim duties were over: web design. Jack offered his name as an endorsement and referral.

Only Sondra retained her original role, still the HR director, though now directing with amplified vigor. Each day, she left the Seattle office grateful for the second chance, grateful for realized potential in people she held close to her heart, and grateful Jack invested in Seattle.

~

Once again, Jack Geoffrey Merton had found a way to come out on top. Legitimately so, this time.

Six years after the infamous presence training, the officeplex overlooking Elliot Bay hadn't imploded; it had doubled.

On the morning of the installation ceremony of the newly expanded steel-and-glass structure, Jack Merton stood before his leadership team, company-wide employees, and guests to congratulate them on their impeccability, yes, but their wholeness more.

Merton Financial–Seattle had become its best—at all layers—present, visible, and lasting. Their commitment to development had inspired a magnitude, releasing the power of their leadership presence.

And that made Jack perfectly happy.

INDEX

ACKNOWLEDGMENTS

To Megan, my wife. You have not only been the guiding influence for our three children (Matt, Maddie, and Alex), but you have continuously supported me in my entrepreneurial dreams, including this latest project.

To our valued clients, partners, advisors, and mentors who have supported our business and our lives and challenged us to continue bringing more and more. We have learned more from you than you can imagine.

To our team members. Thank you for your support, enthusiasm, and passion to make a difference in the lives of many, including mine.

To Dr. Joy Martin. Without the countless hours of research, dedication to excellence, and collaboration, this story of leadership presence would not have come to completion.

ABOUT THE AUTHOR

Boyd Ober's desire to help others achieve success inspired him to found Leadership Resources and continues to fuel his passion today. Serving as president of the company, he devotes his time to building relationships, coaching and consulting with clients, and strengthening the Leadership Resources team. His guidance and direction have enabled the company to experience steady growth since it began in 2002. By empowering leaders to plan their own paths to success, Ober ensures that each client has the necessary resources to enjoy a fantastic development experience.

Ober is an avid supporter of the local communities of Lincoln and Omaha and has established Leadership Resources as an active member of each city's Chamber of Commerce. He has been the recipient of many awards, including the Leadership Management International's (LMI) World Motivator of the Year Award, American

Marketing Association's Marketer of the Year, 360Solutions President's Club Award, LMI Franchise of the Year, and the LMI Growth Award. Ober is a member of the Leadership Management Institute Collaboration Board, Lincoln Partnership for Economic Development Board, Tabitha Inc. Board, and Foundation for Lincoln Public Schools Board.

Excitement, authentic communication, and passion to make a difference are daily values for Boyd Ober. On a regular basis, he shares his business expertise by providing keynote speeches and facilitation for client and community workshops and seminars. His facilitation skills and the ability to ask the right questions enable participants to successfully focus on what matters most to them and their organization. In response to client needs, Ober recently developed innovative processes on emotional intelligence, driven behavior, and leadership presence.

Ober graduated with a master's degree in economics from South Dakota State University. He and his wife, Megan, have three children: Matt, Maddie, and Alex. In his spare time, he enjoys spending time with his family, traveling, golfing, helping with church activities, and having a good conversation over a cup of coffee.

Praise For Magnitude

"Boyd Ober is a man of integrity and is well-qualified to write on the importance of leadership presence. He exemplifies the five-layer model that he writes about in this book. If you want to take your organization to the next level of success, I recommend you read this book and get copies for every member of your leadership team."

Rex C. Houze, President
Improving Performance & Results
Author of *Developing Personal Leadership*

"Boyd Ober is a leader who begins every day on purpose. A motivator and coach, he's willing to go beyond superficial leadership tips to get at the heart of the matter. He truly walks the talk, being fiercely devoted to his core values, habits, and the goal-planning process. Spend even a few minutes with Boyd, and you'll quickly discover why he's a sought-after coach, advisor, and leadership expert."

Ali Schwanke
Marketing Consultant

"Creating a leadership presence can be difficult as more of our communication is conducted through various technologies. Creating an 'in the moment presence' is key to developing a persona that people want to follow. I have known Boyd for over twenty years, and he has always been 'in the moment' as he interacts with people professionally and socially. His insight into how people can develop and improve their leadership presence is a must read."

Daniel J. Duncan, Executive Director
Nebraska Innovation Campus

"Boyd Ober and his team at Leadership Resources do a masterful job in teaching, coaching, and mentoring individual leaders to thrive through their development processes and, in *Magnitude: Releasing the Power of Your Leadership Presence*, now share their best practices to sharpen leadership acumen with the rest of us. It's an exceptional book from a wonderful man. Recommend it highly."

John O'Leary, President
RisingAbove

"Boyd Ober has been a business partner with C&A Industries, Inc., for over two years. With the rapid growth of our company, it was impossible for our training team to keep up with all of the required development needed. Once I got to the point where I knew I needed to enlist in additional help, Boyd was the first person I thought of. His integrity, servant attitude, and mild—yet challenging—demeanor was exactly what our team needed."

Liz Hall, Executive Director, Training and Development
C&A Industries, Inc.

"Throughout my career, I have worked and served with numerous great leaders. A common thread I have found is that the greatest leaders are people deeply respected for their total leadership package, and especially their ethical foundation. Boyd's book provides an enticing view of how leadership presence is deeper than a sharp appearance and contagious personality. All aspiring leaders should be working on continuous improvement, and Boyd's book provides some great ideas on how to make this happen."

Tom Henning, Chairman, President, CEO
Assurity Life Insurance Company

"Boyd Ober believes in helping others realize their full potential. In fact, he told me he was asked one day if he enjoyed his job. His answer, 'I'm living my dream because I get to change lives every day.' And he meant every word of it! What's even better, he does it by listening to them. He asks question after question until he understands what is important to them, and then he offers sustainable processes to give people a path to follow. Simple. Yet magical."

Julie Gade, Market Manager, General Manager
Digity, Lincoln Radio

"What I love most about Boyd is his ability to identify the unique abilities of leaders and put together a plan to maximize personal and professional growth. By combining personal experience and a network of successful business leaders, Boyd provides invaluable insights on what it takes to effectively lead teams of any size. Boyd has been by my side as a friend and mentor in every step of my entrepreneurial journey, helping me build two businesses and become a better person along the way."

Blake Lawrence, Co-Founder
opendorse and Hurrdat

"I have found Boyd's expertise to be impactful in helping me to achieve my personal best for my team as I strive to lead effectively for my business and community. Boyd is a man of sincerity who can be trusted as you look to refine the way you lead in your organization, community, and family."

Patrick Ricketts, MBA, CFP, President & CFO
Vintage Financial Group, LLC
President of Millard School Board

"Many books have been written on the topic of leadership in a broad sense; until now, no one has broken down the soft skills that impact effective leadership. Understanding the importance of your presence as a leader is as important as the customary leadership skills we all have read about. This is a must read for those who aspire to be a complete leader."

John Oestreich, Regional Vice President

"The lack of leadership presence is profound. More than just how one dresses or shakes hands, presence is the ability to be unencumbered by the distractions of the moment, to take responsibility for actions, and to live from a set of values. As a follower of Boyd's work, I recommend we all pay attention. In a unique way, he helps those who struggle with style, etiquette, communication, gravitas, and character become more effective leaders."

Andrea Fredrickson, President
Revela

"I've worked with Boyd for over ten years, first serving as an employee of a local real estate development company and eventually as the president of my own technology firm. Boyd has a special skill for helping us focus on key habits that maintain our competitive advantage. His staff, peer networks, and written resources have the insight to overcome any business challenge."

Devon R. Seacrest, MLS, El Presidente
Digital Environments

"Boyd and his organization have been key partners in enhancing the leadership skills of our growing base of leaders. Our team of leaders has found the process and principles taught to not only apply to their business lives, yet also have a strong impact on their personal lives. Leadership presence is an important factor in their journey."

Mark Hesser, President
Pinnacle Bank

"People want—no, deserve—to be led by a passionate, credible, and talented leader. In the rapidly changing business environment that has become the new norm, a higher level of leadership presence is essential to navigating and leading the people in your personal and professional life and to sustainable business growth. Boyd Ober not only exemplifies this in his own leadership but has helped countless other leaders grow in this regard."

Josh Berry, Director
Smart Matter
Co-Founder, Family Box

"Boyd Ober is a genius at developing leaders. He is authentic, insightful, and inspiring. You don't have to spend much time around Boyd to realize that when it comes to building leaders, he 'gets it.' He's truly a remarkable leader who epitomizes leadership presence."

Mark Balschweid, PhD
Professor and Department Head
Department of Agricultural Leadership,
Education, and Communication
University of Nebraska–Lincoln

"Boyd was a great asset at Cogit during the 'dot com' boom. Cogit was a B2B Internet Infrastructure Company, a pioneer in the field of 'visitor relationship management,' using best of breed data and analytics to optimize content in real time. Boyd's intelligence quickly made him a subject matter authority and trailblazer in this new field. His integrity opened many relationships of conservative Fortune 1000 companies who thought the 'dot com' era was the Wild West."

Mark Wilcox, President
Swat Team Partners

"It is with enthusiasm that I am able to provide this testimonial. I have known Boyd for many years. Boyd is a person of high integrity and character who is passionate about helping people grow as leaders. Boyd understands that it is not just what you say as a leader but how you lead that makes the true impact in the lives of others. The importance of leadership presence is evident in those who bring an intentionality of providing an environment for influencing others to create success. Boyd is a true leader for creating this environment through his leadership style and his ability to create a truly credible presence for both the individual, as well as an entire team of people."

Barry Lockard, President and CEO
Cornhusker Bank

"My professional relationship with Boyd Ober began several years ago when he was asked to be the keynote speaker at our annual Leadership Conference. Since that time, Boyd has worked closely in a coaching and leadership mentoring role with many individuals in our firm. When I think about what makes great leaders great, I think of Boyd Ober. A man of high integrity and character, he has played a significant role in my personal, as well as professional growth and development as a leader. I know Boyd's work and teachings will continue to provide inspiration and wisdom and make a difference for many years to come."

Cliff Karthauser, Managing Director
Principal Financial Group

"Boyd epitomizes leadership presence. I've known Boyd for over twenty years as a friend, coworker, peer, and co-owner. I admire how he conducts himself in all aspects of his life; this isn't just a work-related matter. It has had, and continues to have, a significant impact on the success of everyone around him, including our company, Leadership Resources."

Dan Sedor, Executive Vice President, Implementation Team
Leadership Resources

"There is no other single factor that impacts business results greater than that of leadership. Leadership creates culture, and culture creates the norms and behaviors that produce the results. So if we want a great culture with great results, we need great leadership. Boyd nails it with his five-layer model of leadership presence. In classic Boyd Ober fashion, he distills the complicated into easy application. This book will be the new benchmark for auditing leadership talent in the future."

Dan Krick, Vice President, Organizational Development
Hexagon Composites

"Boyd Ober's leadership skills and practices make him one of the best of the best. As President and CEO of Leadership Resources, Boyd is passionate about creating a continuous, lasting leadership presence among emerging and growing businesses. His successful, multilayered leadership development process has earned him our prestigious Motivator of the Year and Builder of the Year awards. He is truly what we call in our business a 'product of the product.'"

Randy Slechta, CEO
Leadership Management® International, Inc.

"The world is a better place when everyone in it is able to function at the highest degree. Mr. Ober has dedicated his career to assisting everyone he meets to be the most successful person he or she can be; thus, he's directly responsible for the thriving communities in which we live and the thriving companies in which we work. The most vital skill to possess in the coming decades is to THINK. Read this book. Mr. Ober will have succeeded if you become the bearer of the success torch that he has so effectively passed to leaders across the nation."

Derrick Eells, CEO
TenDot

"Boyd Ober is authentic and accountable. He expects no less from his team. This is a must read for today's leaders and tomorrow's."

Douglas E. Flom, Former CEO and President
Midwest Technology Products

"Boyd and his leadership firm have played an integral role in developing our future leaders in our organization. In my personal experience, leadership presence defines you and will reflect your team's performance and overall success of your business. Boyd's five-layer model speaks to his own character and high standard as a business partner and good friend."

Steve Hilton, General Manager
John Q. Hammons Hotels and Resorts

"Leadership is one of the most widely discussed topics in American business. It is also one of the most important issues. Boyd, through his keen understanding of leadership principles and personal commitment, has helped both emerging and seasoned leaders hone their talents. As a result, he has had a significant positive impact on numerous businesses and organizations."

Marc LeBaron, Chairman and CEO
Lincoln Industries

"Ten years ago, I was ambitious, passionate, hard-working, and determined, but I found myself spinning in circles and coming up short in the pursuit of my goals. Boyd Ober helped channel this energy into positive results through improved leadership skills of focus, prioritization, and communication. Ultimately, this helped me achieve a lifelong dream of opening my own business, KidGlov, and balancing my work with family and personal time for ultimate success."

Lyn Wineman, President, Chief Strategist
KidGlov Brand Advancement

"Leadership presence is critical to a leader's success. Boyd Ober has proven this through his own leadership, time and time again, just how powerful 'nailing' leadership presence is! Boyd's circle of influence is big, wide, and varied because he has mastered this five-layer model, and he knows how much of each to bring forth when. Boyd's ability to break the secret sauce of leadership presence down into the key areas of style, etiquette, communication, gravitas, and character makes this book a great tool for someone looking to nail leadership presence and a wonderful reminder for leaders who have (or think they have) it!"

Christie Hinrichs, President, CEO
Tabitha

"*Magnitude: Releasing the Power of Your Leadership Presence* meets a growing need in today's world. More and more, business owners and leaders are distracted by the busyness of tactical demands and fail to leverage the unique but subtle power that lies within. Centered, intentional leadership that displays genuine and impactful influence is an intangible, yet invaluable capacity. Boyd has so generously contributed to my personal growth and success as a leader, and I am eternally grateful for his wisdom and example. He understands, and has mastered, the practice of leadership presence and has a unique gift for teaching the same to others."

Laurie K. Baedke, FACHE, FACMPE, President, Founder
Baedke + Co. Consulting

"At the beginning of the day, it's about leadership. At the end of the day, it's about leadership. Leadership is about inspiring, motivating, coaching, executing, and delivering results. It's easy to lead during good times. However, the true measure of leadership is when times are tough."

Kimberly D. Goins, Director of Volunteers
Tabitha

"Boyd Ober's leadership development processes are the essence creating a pipeline of leaders who are ready to handle business challenges in all climates. Boyd is the epitome of leadership, and he models behaviors for others to follow. His impact on leadership is irrefutable, as depicted by the students that have graduated from his training and their contributions to businesses."

Anthony L. Goins ("Tony"), Executive Vice President
Cabela's CLUB

"Boyd Ober's personal mission is to empower others to plan, develop, and achieve their own journey to success. Boyd is able to work with people, helping them discover the skills and tools they have, as well as those skills and tools they need for their own personal and professional growth and success. Because of his achievements and abilities, Boyd is deeply respected in this field, and his national awards and notoriety are a testament to his expertise as a coach and advisor in the leadership field. I would recommend this book to anyone committed to getting to the next level in either a personal or professional way."

Tim Clare, Partner, Rembolt Ludtke LLP
Regent, University of Nebraska

About Leadership Resources

WHO WE HELP

Like the fictitious character of Glen O'Brien, Leadership Resources is the trusted advisor of growth companies, aligning business strategy with emerging leadership development and creating successful plans for individuals and organizations alike.

WHO WE ARE

We are a leadership development company that identifies emerging leaders, aligns personal goals with corporate vision, and develops leaders within organizations for future impact that drives results and increases cultural fit.

The company is located in Lincoln, Nebraska.

WHAT WE BELIEVE

- **Honesty and Integrity**

  Through our respect for others we enter into and maintain business relationships that are mutually beneficial and built on a foundation of trust.

- **Passion to Make a Difference**

  Our fundamental passion is to make a positive impact on the lives of others and our communities.

- **Commitment to Excellence**

  We seek to understand what matters most to our clients and deliver tailored processes to accomplish their objectives.

- **Green and Growing**

  Inherently, no person or organization is perfect. There is always room for improvement. It's not about perfection; it's about progress.

- **Talent**

  It is imperative to recognize and develop the gifts of others while doing the same for ourselves.

- **Balanced Lifestyle**

  We are a product of our process and enthusiastically seek to live a balanced lifestyle by practicing the leadership principles we endorse.

- **Profit**

  Profit is fundamental to operating a successful business in which we maintain respected community and client relationships while providing for our families.

- **Success**

  Success for our clients and us is the progressive realization of worthwhile, predetermined personal goals.

Bring the Book to Life...

DEVELOPING LEADERSHIP PRESENCE

Avoid the traps that Jack Merton fell into. Cultivate your authentic presence as a leader with Leadership Resources's comprehensive series designed to help you create a positive and lasting impression.

LEADERSHIP PRESENCE SPEAKING ENGAGEMENTS

If you would like to set up a speaking engagement for Boyd Ober, please call or e-mail his marketing manager, Beth Bartek at (402) 423-5152 or beth.bartek@LRsuccess.com.

EMERGING LEADER PROCESS

Are you ready to take your leadership to the next level? Engage in the Leadership Resources Emerging Leader Process. Continuous and holistic development designed for the active professional who demonstrates immense potential, gives more than they take, and embodies green and growing.

LRSUCCESSPATH*

A comprehensive leadership development platform allowing you to do what you do best...coach. You and your clients will be able to have clarity on their development plan, progress, and results, which will further reinforce the value you help drive.

STRATEGIC DIRECTION

Development in a vacuum can challenge the performance of even the best leaders. Create alignment in your organization and allow performance to grow.

Leadership Resources

YOUR NEXT LEVEL OF SUCCESS

8535 EXECUTIVE WOODS DRIVE, SUITE 300

LINCOLN, NE 68512

402.423.5152

WE INVITE YOU TO CONTACT US:

FACEBOOK.COM/LEADERSHIPRESOURCESSUCCESS

LINKEDIN.COM/COMPANY/LEADERSHIP-RESOURCES

TWITTER.COM/LR_SUCCESS

WWW.LRSUCCESS.COM

51654971R00141

Made in the USA
Lexington, KY
30 April 2016